TATTING HEARTS

Teri Dusenbury

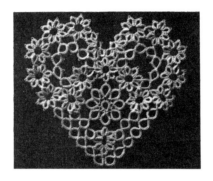

DOVER PUBLICATIONS, INC.
New York

Dedicated to the memory of my dear friend, Mei Sato and my mother, Mildred Gayle Schwegler-Figgins.

To Ollie, for his support, encouragement and inspiration, my heart belongs to you.

Special thanks and credit to Anne Orr for creating the original split ring technique, Mary Sue Kuhn for her work in promoting the technique and Nani Diaz for teaching me how to tat.

Bibliographical Note

Tatting Hearts, first published by Dover Publications, Inc., in 1994, is a revised, corrected and completely reset publication of the following works: *Regal Heart* in *TATtle TALES, Volume One, Issue One*, 1988; *My Fluttering Heart* in *TATtle TALES, Volume Two, Issue Six*, 1989; *Heart Catcher, Queen of Hearts* and *Heart O' Daisies* in *HEARTS*, 1990 (all originally published by Teri Dusenbury, Tacoma, Washington); *To My Hearts Content* and *Heartbreaker* in *HEARTS TOO!*, 1991; *Heartfelt, Cupid's Heart* and *Heartframe* in *TATbit's, Volume One, Issue Two*, 1991; *Heart Blossom* and *Gypsy Heart* in *TATtle TALES, Volume Four, Issue One*, 1992 (all originally published by Teri Dusenbury, Port Orchard, Washington).

Library of Congress Cataloging-in-Publication Data

Dusenbury, Teri.
    Tatting hearts / Teri Dusenbury.
        p.   cm. — (Dover needlework series)
    A revised, corrected republication of patterns originally appearing in various newsletters published by the author from 1988 to 1992.
    ISBN 0-486-28071-3 (pbk.)
    1. Tatting—Patterns. 2. Heart in art. I. Title. II. Series.
TT840.T38D87 1994
746.43'6041—dc20
                                                            94-17257
                                                                CIP

Manufactured in the United States of America
Dover Publications, Inc., 31 East 2nd Street, Mineola, N.Y. 11501

Introduction

How mysteriously the shuttle flies between fingers and thread, creating a unique and precious piece of lace from the mere manipulation of a threaded shuttle!

Tatting is the manipulation of a slip knot, the double stitch, and the variations of it. The double stitch consists of two hitches that, when properly formed, become a slip knot that relies on a internal thread for support. From hitches to stitches come rings, chains, flowers, butterflies and hearts.

Tatting has a rich evolutionary history. Evidence is given in ancient hieroglyphic texts that the early Egyptians practiced a method of forming rings and circles using a shuttle called a *makouk*. With the rise of civilization, knotting (which tatting is said to have derived from) found its way westward from China when the Dutch opened the Middle East to trade. Knotting also utilized a shuttle to manipulate the thread into actual knots, and it became the favorite pastime of the elite in England around the late sixteenth century. It wasn't until 1750 that we find evidence of the true form of tatting. A pair of chair covers by Mary Granville Delany had tatted rings incorporated into the design. In England, between 1846 and 1868, a remarkable woman by the name of Mlle. Elenore Riego de la Branchardière wrote eleven books on tatting. Riego is responsible for much of what is considered the traditional style of tatting practiced today.

The Pilgrims brought tatting to America, where its popularity has waxed and waned throughout the years. Popular women's magazines such as *Peterson's*, *Harper's Bazar* and *Godey's* all regularly published tatting in the mid-1800s, but it wasn't until the early 1900s, with the onset of the ten-cent thread company publication, that tatting enjoyed a fashionable resurgence. Talented designers like Anna Wuerfel Brown, Sophie LaCroix, Mary Fitch, Virginia Snow and Anne Champe Orr are just a few who showcased their talents in unique booklets of tatting designs.

Through the genius of one designer, Anne Orr, tatting evolved one step further with one of the most innovative techniques to be discovered since the true chain was established in 1862–split ring tatting. The technique first appeared in 1923 in a J. & P. Coats publication entitled *Crochet, Cross Stitch and Tatting, Book No. 14*. Of the thirteen edgings shown, twelve utilized the new technique. (There was also a centerpiece design that used split rings.) In each publication that the split ring appeared in, there was one page that carried four little pictured examples and a brief explanation of the technique.

Little fanfare was given to such an important development in tatting's history. Very few patterns implemented the technique following its debut; therefore the technique never really had the opportunity to become an established part of everyday tatting techniques. I have yet to find any designs by other authors that implemented the technique since Orr's last tatting publication in 1958, until a designer named Mary Sue Kuhn published her book, *The Joy of Split Ring Tatting*, in 1984. Kuhn took the original technique and brought it into the light that it deserved. She realized the possibilities that were available if one were to utilize the technique when designing.

After seeing Kuhn's *Six-Pointed Split Ring Tatted Star Ornaments* in 1988, I started to implement the technique in my designs. However, there is a difference between the original Orr method and the split ring technique that I implemented then and teach today. Once again a technique evolves.

Orr's split ring technique requires you to remove the ring from the left hand after the first portion of the ring is tatted. The work is then reversed to finish the bottom/second half of the ring. The stitch Orr refers to as the reverse double stitch is misnamed. Orr was basically tatting a double stitch with one difference: the stitch did not "pop" over but was made with the second shuttle's thread and slid into place. There was no actual reversing of the hitches to justify calling it a reverse double stitch.

I have found that it is not necessary to reverse your work to complete the bottom/second half of the split ring nor to reverse your work to tat chains. I also believe that tatting is meant to have a wrong and right side. I've developed a technique called "directional tatting" that enables you to tat in a way that will have your hitches appearing in proper order even when you've had to reverse your work to tat. I'm also the author of a technique called "stacking" that enables you to give tatting a three-dimensional look. Tatted butterflies never looked so real!

I do not give any directions for the traditional method of tatting. It is my belief that the traditional method is an advanced form of manipulation and should only be used by an experienced tatter. If you are new to tatting and are just trying to learn the basic slip knot, I've shown the easiest method I know of to better explain how to manipulate the shuttle and thread. Shuttle size and thread type are purely the choice of the individual using them.

It is my hope that this book will encourage the designer who resides in us all to blossom, and create more patterns for the practitioners of tatting to enjoy.

TERI DUSENBURY

Abbreviations and Explanations

CTM = Continuous Thread Method. Using two shuttles, fill one shuttle and place that shuttle down. Pull enough thread off the ball to fill the second shuttle. Cut the thread from the ball and fill the second shuttle. You will be tatting from the center of the thread. This eliminates two thread ends that would have to be rethreaded into the lace upon completion. The CTM is used primarily in two shuttle tatting.

DR = Directional Ring. Term used when tatting a ring on the reverse (wrong) side of the lace. You execute the hitches in a manner that will have the hitches facing the proper direction on the front of the work. Instead of tatting the double stitch, which would appear in the wrong sequence on the front of the work, you start the ring with the second hitch of the double stitch, then work the required number of double stitches, minus one. End the sequence with the first hitch of the double stitch. Bring the shuttle through the ring to the right side of the work before closing the ring. Directional rings are used primarily in conjunction with split ring patterns.

LHK = Lark's Head Knot. Unlike the reverse double stitch, this stitch does not pop over. When executing the lark's head knot, you work the second hitch and then the first hitch just as you do with the reverse double stitch; however, the hitches are formed with the shuttle thread (S2) and slid into place. The lark's head knot is used primarily in split ring tatting, but can also be utilized in tatting chains.

Lock Stitch. The lock stitch is used to lock the internal thread into place. The lock stitch is formed with the shuttle thread. The thread is pulled down through the top of the picot (instead of up through the bottom of a picot as in ring joins). The shuttle is slipped through the loop and then the loop is pulled taut. A lock stitch does not count as any hitch or stitch. The lock stitch is used primarily in chain tatting joins.

RDS = Reverse Double Stitch. Similar to the double stitch. The double stitch consists of two hitches; when executing the RDS you work the second hitch first and the first hitch last. The hitches "pop" over just as the double stitch hitches do. The RDS is primarily used in chain tatting and eliminates the need to reverse your work to tat a chain.

RW = Reverse Work. Reverse work is used primarily with directional rings.

Stacking. Technique that uses the stacking of rings to give tatting a three-dimensional effect. Method is accomplished in one round.

SR = Split Ring. A split ring is tatted with two shuttles. The top/first part of the ring is tatted with shuttle one, using the double stitch. The bottom/second part of the ring is tatted with shuttle two using the lark's head knot.

S1 = Shuttle one.
S2 = Shuttle two.
S3 = Shuttle three.
R = Ring.
- = Picot.
p = Picot.
+ = Join.
j = Join.
* = Indicates where the pattern repeat starts and ends.
. = Close ring or end of chain.

Pattern Script

The instructions for all of the hearts are written in the same manner. The following examples will help you understand the format used.

S1: R5-5-5-5. Translates to: use shuttle one to execute the stitches. Ring of five double stitches, picot, five double stitches, picot, five double stitches, picot, five double stitches, close ring. A period at the end of a sequence means to close the ring.

S1: R5 + (j to last p worked)5-5 + (j to first p worked of first ring)5. There are now two plus signs where dashes once stood. The plus sign stands for a joined picot, and there are detailed explanations of where to join the picot in parentheses following every + sign.

Chain RDS 5-5. Translates to: Make a chain of five reverse double stitches, picot, five reverse double stitches. All chains are tatted using the rds unless otherwise noted.

RW DR S2: R5-5-5-5. RW Translates to: reverse work, work a directional ring using shuttle two to execute the stitches. The script given tells how the stitches will look on the front of the work. You execute the hitches in a manner that will have the hitches facing the proper direction on the front of the work. Instead of tatting the double stitch, which would appear in the wrong sequence on the front of the work, you start the ring with the second hitch of the double stitch, then work the required number of double stitches, minus one (in this case it would be four whole double stitches), end the sequence with the first hitch of the double stitch, picot, second hitch, four complete double stitches, first hitch, picot, second hitch, four complete double stitches, first hitch, four complete double stitches, second hitch. Don't forget to bring the shuttle through the ring to the right side of the work before closing. Reverse work.

SR Sl: R5-5, S2: LHK 5-5. Translates to: split ring, shuttle one, ring of five double stitches, picot, five double stitches, shuttle two, five lark's head knots, picot, five lark's head knots, close ring.

Schematics

Schematic diagrams are given with each heart to further clarify the instructions for you. Always refer to these diagrams as you follow the script. The following examples will help you understand the diagrams.

The first step of the pattern Queen of Hearts requires that you tat a motif consisting of eight rings. Figure one's schematic shows numbers placed throughout the first ring. The numbers denote the number of double stitches required per sequence to complete the ring. Each consecutive ring's numerical sequence is the same. The script would read S1: R3-5-1-1-5-3.

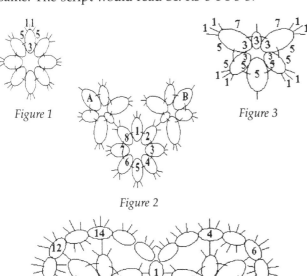

Figure 1

Figure 2

Figure 3

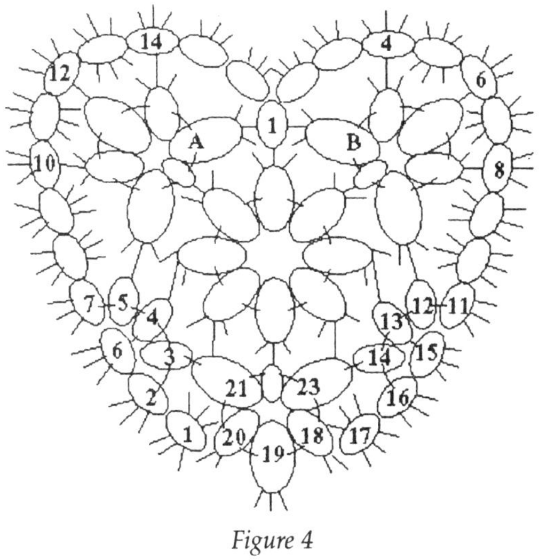

Figure two's schematic of the pattern Queen of Hearts shows that step one's motif consisted of eight rings. The numbers inside the daisy motif denote the sequence in which the rings are tatted. Also shown are the placement of step two's butterfly motifs A and B.

The second step of the pattern Queen of Hearts requires that you tat motifs A and B. Figure three's schematic shows numbers placed throughout the rings. The numbers denote the number of double stitches needed to complete each ring.

Figure four's schematic of the pattern Queen of Hearts shows step three's and step four's ring placement. The numbers inside the rings denote the sequence in which the rings are tatted.

The Third Shuttle Dilemma

Figure five's schematic of the pattern Queen of Hearts shows a close up of the techniques used to complete the half daisy. For ring fifteen, which is a split ring, you need to introduce a third shuttle into the tatting in order to complete the split ring. The second shuttle does not line up properly with the first shuttle, so it cannot be used to complete this ring. The third shuttle is manipulated just as the second shuttle would have been, using the lark's head knot. Once the bottom/second part of

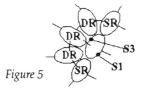

Figure 5

the ring is completed, cut the third shuttle from the thread. There is no need to knot the third shuttle threads, but they will need to be worked into the lace upon completion. The sixteenth ring is tatted with the first and second shuttle.

Getting Started

The key elements to the success of any of the heart projects are good light, a quiet span of time and patience. If you are not familiar with the terminology or the new techniques, take the time to review and practice the examples given before attempting any heart motif.

Each motif is categorized by a skill level. Once you are familiar with the terminology and techniques and have practiced tatting from a scripted pattern, you should try the novice level patterns. After you are completely confident with the concepts used and have successfully tatted the novice patterns, you should attempt the intermediate level. After tatting the intermediate level motifs you will have mastered the techniques. The advanced level motifs won't seem beyond your skill level at this point.

Shuttle size and thread types are purely the choice of the individual using them. All examples were tatted using a mercerized 20-gauge, 3-ply cotton thread.

Figure 4

Finishing Touches

Knot all ends where two threads meet. Rethread all knotted ends back through the lace using a needle threader. Be sure to pull the end threads through as many stitches as possible before cutting off excess thread. It is a good idea to rethread your ends before ironing any piece of lace. The heat from the iron dulls the thread, making it harder to slip the thread through the finished stitches.

Lightly iron on the wrong side of the lace, using a spray starch for a firmer heart. A commercial stiffener should be used for the mobile hearts. Silver filament thread was used to string the hearts for the mobile.

Tatting Basics

Learning To Tat—The Reverse Riego Way

Wrap the thread around your left hand to form a ring and pinch closed with your forefinger and thumb. Hold the shuttle in the right hand. (The shuttle should be held in the right hand even if you write with your left hand.) The shuttle is pinched between the forefinger and thumb of the right hand with the hook or point at the top.

The thread wrapped around your left hand that is pinched between the thumb and forefinger is called the *ring thread*. The thread that comes out from under the thumb and is connected to the shuttle is called the *shuttle thread (Fig. 1)*.

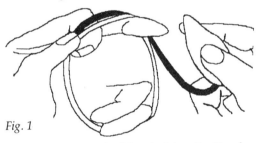

Fig. 1

The first hitch of the double stitch is tatted by draping the shuttle thread over the third finger of the left hand, behind the ring thread. Pointing the shuttle away from you, push the shuttle from in front of the ring thread, back between the third and ring finger of the left hand *(Fig. 2)*.

Fig. 2

Pull the shuttle to the right until the hitch "pops" over *(Figs. 3 & 4)*.

Using the middle finger of your left hand, pull the hitch up and to the left, bringing the hitch taut *(Fig. 5)*.

This is referred to as the *first hitch*. Hold the hitch under the thumb and forefinger of the left hand.

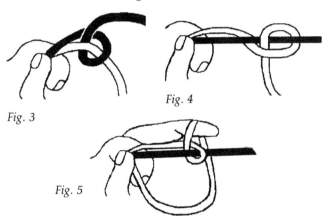

Fig. 3   *Fig. 4*

Fig. 5

The second hitch of the double stitch is tatted by draping the shuttle thread in front of the ring thread. Pointing the shuttle toward you, push the shuttle between the third and ring finger of the left hand from behind the ring thread to the front *(Fig.6)*.

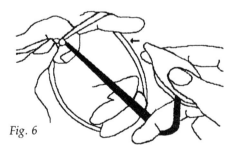

Fig. 6

Pull the shuttle thread to the right until the hitch "pops" over *(Fig. 7)*.

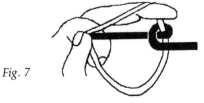

Fig. 7

Using the middle finger of your left hand, pull the hitch up and to the left, bringing the hitch taut and next to the first hitch, completing the double stitch. This is referred to as the *second hitch (Fig. 8)*.

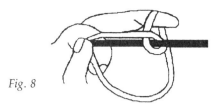

Fig. 8

The Double Stitch

The double stitch consists of the first and second hitch worked in that order.

This is how the double stitch looks when tatted correctly. A good test is to pull the shuttle thread to see if the ring thread still moves freely. If the thread does not move then a mistake has been made (*Fig. 9*).

Fig. 9

Picots

Picots are loops of thread that rest on top of the double stitches. They are easily made by leaving a space between the last hitch of a double stitch and the first hitch of the next double stitch (*Figs. 10 & 11*).

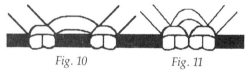

Fig. 10   *Fig. 11*

Joins

Ring joins are made by slipping the ring thread up through the bottom of a prior ring picot. Pull a loop back up through the picot. Bring the shuttle through the loop; pull the loop taut. Tat a regular double stitch. The join is never counted as a stitch nor is it considered the first hitch of the next double stitch (*Fig. 12*).

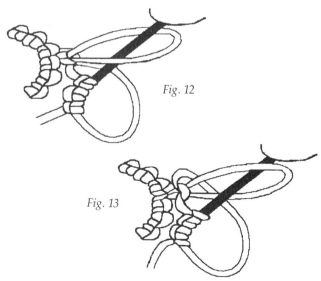

Fig. 12

Fig. 13

Directional ring joins are made by slipping the ring thread down through the top of a prior ring picot. Pull a loop back down through the picot; bring the shuttle

through the loop; pull the loop taut. Tat the second hitch of the double stitch. The join of a directional ring is never counted as a stitch nor is it considered any hitch of the double stitch (*Fig. 13*).

Lock stitch joins are used to lock the internal thread into place when joining a chain to a picot. The lock stitch is formed with the shuttle thread. Pull the shuttle thread down through the top of the picot (instead of up through the picot loop like a normal chain join); slip the shuttle through the loop and then pull the loop taut. The thread that holds the stitches is held into place with a locked stitch, giving the chain a more uniform appearance. The lock stitch join is never counted as a stitch nor is it considered any hitch of the double stitch (*Fig. 14*).

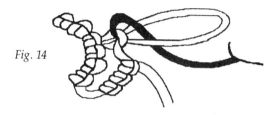

Fig. 14

The Reverse Double Stitch

It is no longer necessary to reverse your lace to tat chains when you use the reverse double stitch. The reverse double stitch consists of the two hitches of the double stitch–the second hitch and the first, in that order. The hitches "pop" over just as the double stitch hitches do.

DO NOT REVERSE YOUR WORK! Wrap the ball thread around your hand securing the thread to the little finger (just as you would have secured the thread if you had reversed your work to chain). Drape the shuttle thread in front of the secured ball thread. Instead of tatting the first hitch of the double stitch, you tat the second hitch. Pointing the shuttle toward you, push the shuttle between the third and ring finger of the left hand from behind the chain thread to the front (*Figs. 15 & 16*).

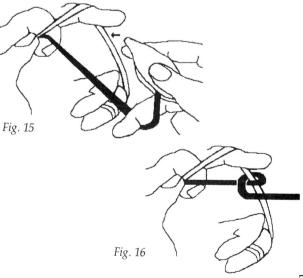

Fig. 15

Fig. 16

Pull the shuttle to the right until the hitch "pops" over (just like the hitches do when tatting the double stitch.) The hitch is made with the ball thread and is carried upon the shuttle thread. The tricky part is getting the starting chain hitch taut and close to the base of the ring; this hitch may take a bit more manipulation to place than consecutive hitches *(Figs. 17 & 18).*

hitch taut and next to the prior hitch to complete the stitch. This stitch is referred to as the true *reverse double stitch (Figs. 19, 20, 21 & 22).*

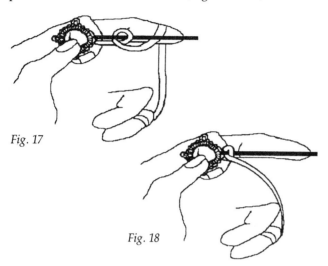

Fig. 17

Fig. 18

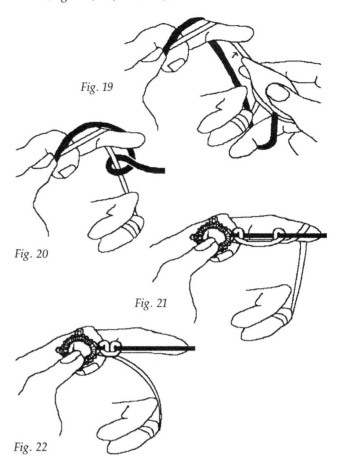

Fig. 19

Fig. 20

Fig. 21

Fig. 22

For the final hitch of the reverse double stitch, drape the shuttle thread over the third finger of the left hand, behind the secured ball thread. Pointing the shuttle away from you, push the shuttle from in front of the chain thread, back between the third and ring finger of the left hand. Pull the shuttle thread to the right until the hitch "pops" over just like the prior hitch. Bring this

Tatting Techniques

Split Ring Tatting

A split ring is a ring tatted with two shuttles. The top/first part of the ring is tatted with shuttle one using the double stitch. The bottom/second part of the ring is tatted with shuttle two using the lark's head knot.

Use two shuttles wound CTM. The script reads: SR Sl: R5-5, S2: LHK 5-5. This translates to split ring, shuttle one, ring of five double stitches, picot, five double stitches. The first part of the ring is complete. Drape shuttle one behind the fingers of the left hand. Pick up shuttle two; the script continues with shuttle two, five lark's head knots, picot, five lark's head knots, close ring.

It does not matter how you hold the shuttle or in what style you execute the double stitch (the traditional or reverse Riego style) for the first part of the ring. However, it is easier to manipulate the shuttle if you tat the lark's head knot using the reverse Riego style of holding the shuttle.

Tat the first part of the split ring with shuttle one: SR S1: R5-5 *(Fig. 1).*

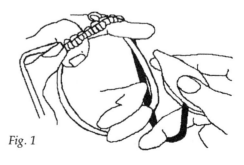

Fig. 1

S2: LHK 5-5. The bottom/second part of the ring is always tatted using the lark's head knot. The lark's head knot does not pop over like the reverse double stitch, but is made with the second shuttle's thread and is slid into place. Shuttle two is placed over/under the ring thread and over the shuttle thread.

Pull the shuttle down and to the left; slide the first hitch next to the first double stitch tatted (*Figs. 2 & 3*).

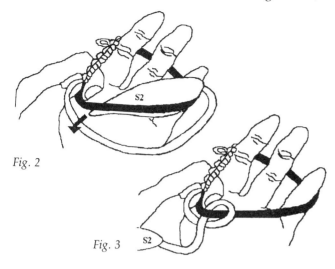

Fig. 2

Fig. 3

The shuttle is then worked away from you and under/over the ring thread and under the shuttle thread. Pull the shuttle down and to the left, sliding the second hitch into place. Pull on shuttle one's thread to see if the ring thread still moves and a mistake has not been made (*Figs. 4 & 5*).

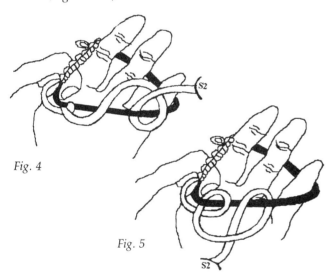

Fig. 4

Fig. 5

Directional Tatting

When you reverse your work and tat a double stitch, the hitches are in reverse order on the front of your lace. With directional tatting, you tat the first and second hitches of the double stitch in reverse order to achieve a complete double stitch on the front of your lace.

The double stitch consists of two hitches: the first hitch (the shuttle away from you) and the second hitch (the shuttle toward you) (*front view*). When you reverse your work, the double stitch is seen as the second hitch followed by the first hitch (*back view*) (Fig. 6).

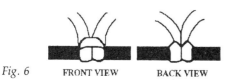

Fig. 6   FRONT VIEW   BACK VIEW

Patterns that utilize directional ring tatting show the script written as the stitches will appear on the front of the lace. The key is **RW DR**, which requires you to follow the formula given below in order to have all the stitches facing the front of the lace.

The best way to understand directional tatting is by tatting the following examples:

In the first example, the script reads **RW DR** S2: R5-5-5-5. **RW**. You will need to break that first sequence of double stitches down in your mind to read second hitch, four complete double stitches, first hitch. It is helpful to remember that each sequence starts with the second hitch, ends with the first hitch and the number of complete double stitches is one less than the total number. This is how the pattern script would read if it were written to show how the stitches would appear on the reverse side of the lace. **RW DR** S2: R2h, 4ds, 1h-2h, 4ds, 1h-2h, 4ds, 1h-2h, 4ds, 1h. **RW**. (Key: 1h = first hitch, 2h = second hitch, ds = double stitch)

Directional rings are usually tatted with the second shuttle; for this example, you use only one shuttle. Wrap the shuttle thread around your left hand to form a ring. Instead of tatting the first hitch of the double stitch, you tat the second hitch of the double stitch, four complete double stitches and then the first hitch of the double stitch. This is one sequence: S2: R5. The front of the work will show five complete double stitches. To make picots, leave a space between the first and second hitch of the double stitch. Continue in pattern. After completion of the last sequence of five stitches, remember to bring the shuttle through the ring to the front of the lace (*Fig. 7*). Reverse work so that the front is now facing you; close ring.

For example two, you will be using two shuttles wound CTM. The pattern script will read: S1: R5-5-5-5. *S1: R5 + (j to last p worked)5-5-5.* Repeat once more. (3 rings total.) **RW DR** S2: R5 + (j to first p of first ring)5-5-5. S2: R5 + (j to last p worked)5-5-5. **RW** (5 rings total.) SR S1: R5 + (j to p of last S1 ring)5, S2: LHK

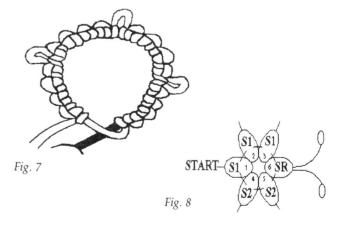

Fig. 7

START—⟨S1⟩⟨S1⟩ ⟨S1⟩ ⟨SR⟩ ⟨S2⟩⟨S2⟩

Fig. 8

5 + (j to p of last DR)5. End of example (6 rings total) (*Fig. 8*).

Directional ring joins are made by slipping the ring thread down through the top of a prior ring picot. Pull a loop back down through the picot, bring the shuttle through the loop, pull the loop taut. The join of a directional ring is never counted as a stitch nor is it considered any hitch of the double stitch *(Figs. 9 & 10)*.

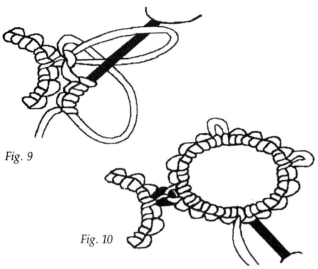

Fig. 9

Fig. 10

Stacking

Stacking is a technique in which you tat rings one on top of the other to achieve a three-dimensional effect. The best way to learn how to stack is to tat the following butterfly example.

Ring one–*butt:* R5-5-1-1-5-5 *(Fig. 11)*.

Ring two–*upper left small wing:* R8-1-1-5-3. YOU DO NOT CONNECT THE RING TO ANY PICOTS. Fold this ring down so that the wrong side is facing up *(Fig. 12)*.

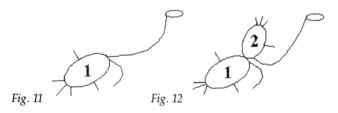

Fig. 11   Fig. 12

Ring three–*lower left small wing:* R5 + (j to last p of ring one)3-1-1-5-3. Push the second ring in front of the third ring *(Fig. 13)*.

Ring four–*upper left large wing:* R3 + (j to last p of ring two)5-1-1-10-3. Fold both connected wings down so that the wrong side is facing up *(Fig. 14)*.

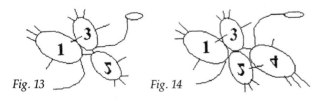

Fig. 13   Fig. 14

Ring five–*lower left large wing:* R3 + (j to last p of ring three)5-1-1-10-3. Fold both connected wings up so that they are stacked on each other *(Fig. 15)*.

Ring six–*head:* R3 + (j to last p of rings four and five)1-1-3 *(Fig. 16)*.

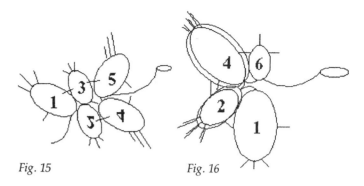

Fig. 15   Fig. 16

Ring seven–*lower right large wing:* R3 + (j to last p of ring six)10-1-1-5-3 *(Fig. 17)*.

Ring eight–*upper right large wing:* R3 + (j to same p of ring six that you joined ring seven to)10-1-1-5-3 *(Fig. 18)*.

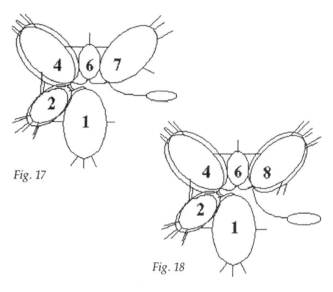

Fig. 17

Fig. 18

Ring nine–*lower right small wing:* R3 + (j to last p of ring seven)5-1-1-3 + (j to first p of ring one)5 *(Fig. 19)*.

Ring ten–*upper right small wing:* R3 + (j to last p of ring eight)5-1-1-8. End off *(Fig. 20)*.

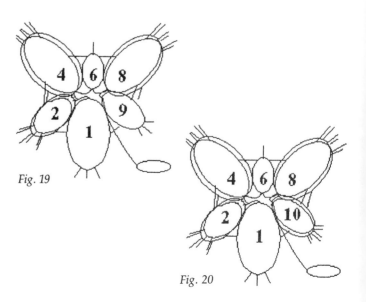

Fig. 19

Fig. 20

Regal Heart

Novice skill level.
Materials: 2 shuttles, Size 20-gauge 3-ply thread.

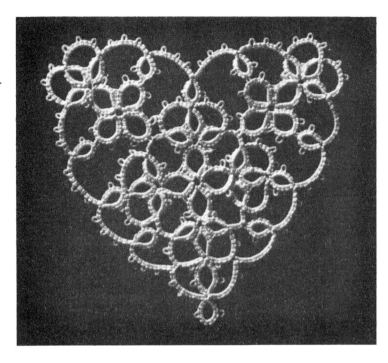

Center Motif (Fig. 1)

Wind one shuttle only.
R4-3-3-3-3-4.
R4 + (j to last p worked)3-3-3-3-4. Repeat once more.
R4 + (j to last p worked)3-3-3-3 + (j to first picot of first ring)4. End off.

Second Round (Fig. 2)

Wind one shuttle leaving ball thread attached.

Three-Ring Cluster:
R4-3 + (j to center p of any first round ring)3-4.
Chain RDS 3-3-3-3.
R4 + (j to last p worked of last ring)3 + (j in same center p as last ring)3-4.
Chain RDS 3-3-3-3.
R4 + (j to last p worked of last ring)3 + (j in same center p as last ring)3-4.
Chain RDS 3-3.

Three-Ring Cluster:
*R4-3 + (j to center p of next first round ring)3-4.
Chain RDS 3-3-3-3.
R4 + (j to last p worked of last ring)3 + (j in same center p as last ring)3-4.
Chain RDS 3-3-3-3.

R4 + (j to last p worked of last ring)3 + (j in same center p as last ring)3-4.
Chain RDS 3-3.* Repeat 2x more. End off. Join last chain to base of first ring and beginning chain.

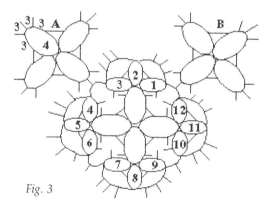

Fig. 3

Clover Motifs (Fig. 3)

Wind one shuttle only.

Left A Clover Motif:

R4-3-3-3-3-4.
R4 + (j to last p worked)3-3 + (j to chain containing one picot)3-3-4.
R4 + (j to last p worked)3-3-3-3-4.
R4 + (j to last p worked)3-3-3-3 + (j to first p worked of first ring)4. End off.

Right B Clover Motif:

R4-3-3-3-3-4.
R4 + (j to last p worked)3-3 + (j to next one-picot chain from previously joined motif)3-3-4.
R4 + (j to last p worked)3-3-3-3-4.
R4 + (j to last p worked)3-3-3-3 + (j to first p worked of first ring)4. End off.

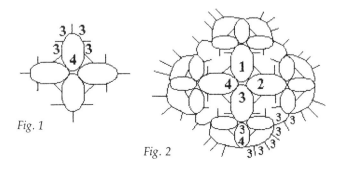

Fig. 1

Fig. 2

11

Regal Border *(Fig. 4)*

Using CTM wind two shuttles.

S1: R4-3-3 + (j to space below second ring of three-ring cluster at bottom of heart)3-3-4.

RW DR S2: R4-3-3-4. **RW**

Chain RDS 3-3-3-3 + (join with a lock stitch in second p of next chain)3-3-3-3.

S1: R4-3 + (j to next one-picot chain)3-4.

Chain RDS 3-3-3-3.

S1: R4-3 + (j to base of second ring of the next three-ring cluster)3-4.

Chain RDS 3-3-3-3.

S1: R4-3 + (j to center p of next ring of right clover motif)3-4.

Chain RDS 3-3-3-3.

S1: R4-3 + (j to center p of next ring of right clover motif)3-4.

Chain RDS 3-3-3-3.

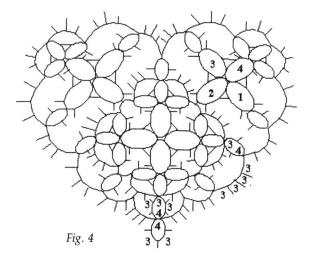

Fig. 4

S1: R4 + (j to last p worked of last ring)3 + (j in same center p as last ring)3-4.

Chain RDS 3-3-3-3.

S1: R4 + (j to last p worked of last ring)3 + (j in same center p as last ring)3-4.

Chain RDS 3-3-3-3.

S1: R4-3 + (j to center p of next ring of right clover motif)3-4.

Chain RDS 3-3-3-3.

S1: R4-3 + (j to base of second ring of next three-ring cluster)3-4.

Chain RDS 3-3-3-3.

S1: R4-3 + (j to center p of next ring of left clover motif)3-4.

Chain RDS 3-3-3-3.

S1: R4-3 + (j to center p of next ring of left clover motif)3-4.

Chain RDS 3-3-3-3.

S1: R4 + (j to last p worked of last ring)3 + (j in same center p as last ring)3-4.

Chain RDS 3-3-3-3.

S1: R4 + (j to last p worked of last ring)3 + (j in same center p as last ring)3-4.

Chain RDS 3-3-3-3.

S1: R4-3 + (j to center p of next ring of left clover motif)3-4.

Chain RDS 3-3-3-3.

S1: R4-3 + (j to base of second ring of next three-ring cluster)3-4.

Chain RDS 3-3-3-3.

S1: R4-3 + (j to next one-picot chain)3-4.

Chain RDS 3-3-3-3 + (join with a lock stitch in center p of chain)3-3-3-3. End off. Join last chain in base of first ring.

Heart O' Daisies

Novice skill level.

Materials: 2 shuttles, Size 20-gauge 3-ply thread.

Daisies *(Fig. 1)*

Daisy One:

Using CTM wind two shuttles.

12

S1: R5-5-5-5.

S1: R5 + (j to last p worked)5-5-5. Repeat 5x more.

SR S1: R5 + (j to last p worked)5, S2: LHK 5 + (j to first p worked of first ring)5. (8 rings)

SR S1: R3-3, S2: LHK 3-3.

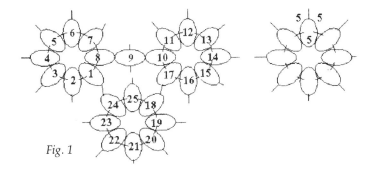

Fig. 1

Daisy Two:

SR S1: R5-5, S2: LHK 5-5.

S1: R5 + (j to last S1 p worked)5-5-5. Repeat 5x more.

SR S1: R5 + (j to last p worked)5, S2: LHK 5 + (j to LHK p of ring 10)5.

Daisy Three:

SR S1: R5-5, S2: LHK 5-5.

S1: R5 + (j to last S1 p)5-5-5. Repeat 4x more.

S1: R5 + (j to last p worked)5 + (j to center p of first ring)5-5.

S1: R5 + (j to last p worked)5-5 + (j to LHK p of ring 18)5. End off.

Heart Point *(Fig. 2)*

Wind one shuttle leaving ball thread connected.

R3-3-3-3.

Chain RDS 5 + (j to center p of ring 21 of daisies).

R3 + (j to last p worked)3-3-3. Repeat 2x more.

Chain RDS 5.

R3 + (j to last p worked)3-3-3. End off.

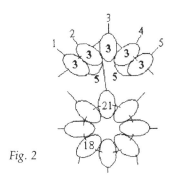

Fig. 2

Heart Border *(Fig. 3)*

Using CTM wind two shuttles.

S1: R3-3 + (j to first p, ring 1 of heart point)3 + (j to center p of ring 20 of daisies)3.

SR S1: R3-3, S2: LHK 3-3. Repeat 2x more.

S1: R3-3 + (j to center p of ring 15)3-3.

Chain RDS 2-2-2-2.

S1: R3-3 + (j to center p of ring 14)3-3.

Chain RDS 2-2-2-2.

S1: R3 + (j to last p of last ring worked)3 + (j to center p of ring 14)3-3.

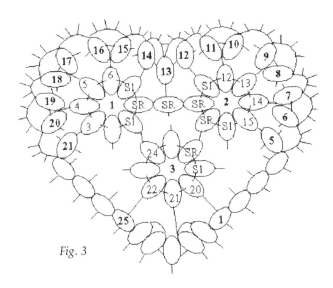

Fig. 3

Chain RDS 2-2-2-2.

S1: R3-3 + (j to center p of ring 13)3-3.

Chain RDS 2-2-2-2.

S1: R3 + (j to last p of last ring worked)3 + (j to center p of ring 13)3-3.

Chain RDS 2-2-2-2.

S1: R3-3 + (j to center p of ring 12)3-3.

Chain RDS 2-2-2-2.

S1: R3 + (j to last p of last ring worked)3 + (j to center p of ring 12)3-3.

Chain RDS 2-2-2-2.

S1: R3-3 + (j to center p of ring 11)3-3.

Chain RDS 2-2-2-2.

S1: R3 + (j to last p of last ring worked)3 + (j to center p of ring 9)3-3.

Chain RDS 2 + (j to last p of last chain worked)2-2-2.

Sl: R3 + (j to last p of last ring worked)3 + (j to center p of ring 7)3-3.

Chain RDS 2-2-2-2.

S1: R3-3 + (j to center p of ring 6)3-3.

Chain RDS 2-2-2-2.

S1: R3 + (j to last p of last ring worked)3 + (j to center p of ring 6)3-3.

Chain RDS 2-2-2-2.

S1: R3-3 + (j to center p of ring 5)3-3.

Chain RDS 2-2-2-2.

S1: R3 + (j to last p of last ring worked)3 + (j to center p of ring 5)3-3.

Chain RDS 2-2-2-2.

S1: R3-3 + (j to center p of ring 4)3-3.

Chain RDS 2-2-2-2.

S1: R3 + (j to last p of last ring worked)3 + (j to center p of ring 4)3-3.

Chain RDS 2-2-2-2.

S1: R3-3 + (j to center p of ring 3)3-3.

SR S1: R3-3, S2: LHK 3-3. Repeat 2x more.

SR S1: R3 + (j to center p of ring 22)3, S2: LHK 3-3. End off. Join in last p of heart point.

Heart Catcher

Novice/intermediate skill level.
Materials: 2 shuttles, Size 20-gauge 3-ply thread, clear
nylon filament thread.

Heart Frame *(Fig. 1)*

Using CTM wind two shuttles.
S1: R3-3-3-3.
SR S1: R2-1-1-2, S2: LHK 6. Repeat 10x more. (12 rings
total)

Butterfly *(Fig. 2)*:

Right large wing: SR S1: R1-5-3, S2: LHK 1-10-3.
Right small wing: S1: R3 + (j to last S1 p of split
ring)5-1-1-3-5.
Butt: S1: R5 + (j to last p worked)5-1-1-5-5.
Left small wing: S1: R5 + (j to last p worked)3-1-1-5-3.
Head: **RW DR** S2: R3 + (j to LHK p of split ring)1-1-3. **RW**
Left large wing: SR S1: R3 + (j to p of right small wing)5-1,
S2: LHK 3 + (j to p of head)10-1.

SR S1: R2-1-1-2, S2: LHK 6. Repeat 9x more.
S1: R2-1-1-2 + (j to base of first ring)6. End off.

Ring three—*lower left small wing:* R5 + (j to last p of ring
one)3-1-1-5-3.
Ring four—*lower left large wing:* R3 + (j to last p of ring
two)5-1-1-10-3.
Ring five—*upper left large wing:* R3 + (j to last p of ring
three)5-1-1-10-3.
Ring six—*head:* R3 + (j in p of both rings four and
five)1-1-3.
Ring seven—*lower right large wing:* R3 + (j to last p of
ring six)10-1-1-5-3.
Ring eight—*upper right large wing:* R3 + (j to last p of
ring six)10-1-1-5-3.
Ring nine—*lower right small wing:* R3 + (j to last p of
ring seven)5-1-1-3 + (j to first p of R1)5.
Ring ten—*upper right small wing:* R3 + (j to last p of ring
eight)5-1-1-4-4. End off.

See Tatting Techniques, p. 10, for complete directions
for stacking.

Tie the stacked butterfly onto second picot of first ring
using clear filament *(Fig. 3)*.

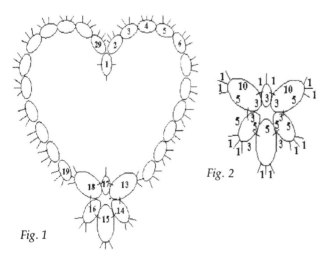

Fig. 1

Fig. 2

Stacked Butterfly

Wind one shuttle only.
Ring one—*butt:* R5-5-1-1-5-5.
Ring two—*upper left small wing:* R4-4-1-1-5-3.

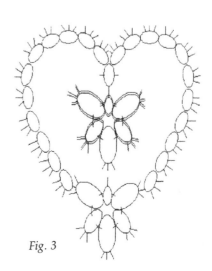

Fig. 3

My Fluttering Heart

Intermediate skill level.
Materials: 3 shuttles, Size 20-gauge 3-ply thread.

Center Motif (*Fig. 1*)

Wind one shuttle only and leave ball thread connected.
R3-3-3-3.
Chain RDS 5-5.
*R3 + (j to last p worked of prior ring)3-3-3.
Chain RDS 5-5.* Repeat 6x more.
R3 + (j to last p worked of prior ring)3-3 + (j to first p worked of first ring)3.
Chain RDS 5-5. (9 rings total) End off. Join to base of first ring.

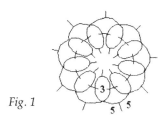

Fig. 1

Upper Butterfly Motifs (*Figs. 2 & 3*)

Wind one shuttle only.

Butterfly A:
Left small wing: R4-4-5-3.
Left large wing: R3 + (j to last p worked)6-8-3.
Head: R3 + (j to last p worked)1 + (j to any p of any chain from center motif)1-3.
Right large wing: R3 + (j to last p worked)8-6-3.
Right small wing: R3 + (j to last p worked)5-4-4. End off.

Butterfly B:
Left small wing: R4-4-5-3.
Left large wing: R3 + (j to last p worked)6-8-3.
Head: R3 + (j to last p worked)1 + (j to second chain p to the right of where butterfly A is connected)1-3.
Right large wing: R3 + (j to last p worked)8-6-3.
Right small wing: R3 + (j to last p worked)5-4-4. End off.

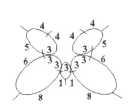

Fig. 2 *Fig. 3*

Outer Cameo Split Ring Border

(*Figs. 4, 5 & 6*)

Using CTM wind two shuttles. Wind one shuttle separately.
S1: R3 + (j to right large wing of butterfly B)3 + (j to chain p of center motif)3 + (j to left large wing of butterfly A)3.
SR S1: R3-3, S2: LHK 3-3. Repeat once more.
SR S1: R3-3, S2: LHK 3 + (j to outer p of right small wing of butterfly B)3.
SR S1: R3-3, S2: LHK 3-3.
SR S1: R3-3, S2: LHK 3 + (j to center p of left small wing of butterfly B)3.
SR S1: R3-3, S2: LHK 3-3.* Repeat 2x more (*Fig. 4*).

Half Daisy (*Fig. 5*):
RW DR S2: R3 + (j to last p worked)3 + (j to left large wing of butterfly B)3-3.
S2: R3 + (j to last p worked)3 + (j to corresponding chain p of center motif)3-3.
S2: R3 + (j to last p worked)3-3-3. **RW**
SR S1: R3-3, using *shuttle three* LHK 3 + (j in base of second directional ring)3. End off S3.
SR S1: R3-3, S2: LHK 3 + (j to last p worked of third directional ring)3.
SR S1: R3-3, S2: LHK 3 + (j to next chain p of center motif)3.
SR S1: R3-3, S2: LHK 3-3. Do not end off.

15

Corner Clover:

SR S1: R3-3-3, S2: LHK 3 + (j to next chain p of center motif).

Chain RDS 5.

S1: R3 + (j to last p worked)3-3-3. Repeat 2x more.

Chain RDS 5 + (j to next chain p of center motif).

SR S1: R3 + (j to last p worked)3-3, S2: LHK 3.

SR S1: R3-3, S2: LHK 3-3.

SR S1: R3-3, S2: LHK 3 + (j to next chain p of center motif)3.

SR S1: R3-3, S2: LHK 3-3.

RW DR S2: R3 + (j to last p worked)3-3-3.

S2: R3 + (j to last p worked)3 + (j to next chain p of center motif)3-3.

S2: R3 + (j to last p worked)3 + (j to right large wing of butterfly A)3-3. **RW**

SR S1: R3-3, using *shuttle three* LHK 3 + (j in base of second directional ring)3. End off S3.

SR S1: R3-3, S2: LHK 3 + (j to last p worked of third directional ring)3.

SR S1: R3-3, S2: LHK 3-3. Repeat once more.

SR S1: R3-3, S2: LHK 3 + (j to outer p of right small wing of butterfly A)3.

SR S1: R3-3, S2: LHK 3-3.

SR S1: R3-3, S2: LHK 3 + (j to outer p of left small wing of butterfly A)3.

SR S1: R3-3, S2: LHK 3-3. Repeat once more. End off. Join to base of first ring (*Fig. 6*).

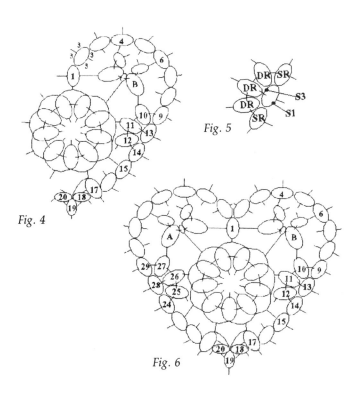

Fig. 4

Fig. 5

Fig. 6

Queen of Hearts

Intermediate skill level.

Materials: 3 shuttles, Size 20-gauge 3-ply thread.

Center Flower Motif *(Fig. 1)*

Wind one shuttle.

R3-5-1-1-5-3.

R3 + (j to last p worked)5-1-1-5-3. Repeat 5x more.

R3 + (j to last p worked)5-1-1-5 + (j to first p of first ring)3. End off. (8 rings)

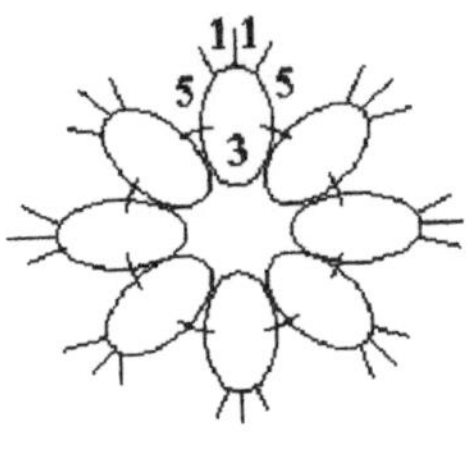

Fig. 1

Butterfly Motifs (*Figs. 2 & 3*)

Wind one shuttle.

Butterfly butt: R5-5-5-5.

Left small wing: R5 + (j to last p worked)3-1-1-5-3.

Left large wing: R3 + (j to last p worked)5-1-1-7-3.

Head: R3 + (j to last p worked)1 + (j to any center p of center flower motif)1-3.

Right large wing: R3 + (j to last p worked)7-1-1-5-3.

Right small wing: R3 + (j to last p worked)5-1-1-3 + (j to first p worked of first ring)5. End off.

Repeat butterfly motif one more time, joining to center p of third ring to either side of last joined motif.

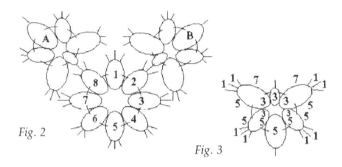

Fig. 2

Fig. 3

Border (*Figs. 4 & 5*)

Using CTM wind two shuttles. Wind one shuttle separately.

Right Side:

S1: R3 + (j to center p of right large wing from right butterfly motif)3 + (j to center p of ring 1 of center flower motif)3 + (j to center p of left large wing from left butterfly motif)3.

SR S1: R2-1-1-2, S2: LHK 6. Repeat once more.

SR S1: R2-1-1-2, S2: LHK 3 + (j to center p of right small wing)3.

SR S1: R2-1-1-2, S2: LHK 2-1-1-2.

S1: R2-1-1-2, S2: LHK 3 + (j to butterfly B's butt)3.

SR S1: R2-1-1-2, S2: LHK 2-1-1-2.

SR S1: R2-1-1-2, S2: LHK 3 + (j to center p of left small wing)3.

SR S1: R2-1-1-2, S2: LHK 2-1-1-2. Repeat once more.

Half Daisy (Fig. 5):

SR S1: R2-1-1-2, S2: LHK 3-3.

RW DR S2: R3 + (j to last p worked)3 + (j to center p of left large wing of butterfly B)3-3.

S2: R3 + (j to last p worked)3 + (j to center p of ring three of center flower motif)3-3.

S2: R3 + (j to last p worked)3-3-3. **RW**

SR S1: R2-1-1-2, using *shuttle three* LHK 3 + (j to base of center DR)3. End off S3.

SR S1: R2-1-1-2, S2: LHK 3 + (j to last p of last DR worked)3.

SR S1: R2-1-1-2, S2: LHK 2-1-1-2.

Butterfly Point:

Right small wing: SR S1: R1-1-3-5, S2: LHK 5-3. End off S2.

Butterfly butt: S1: R5 + (j to last p worked)5-1-1-5-5.

Left small wing: S1: R5 + (j to last p worked)3-1-1-5-3.

Left large wing: S1: R3 + (j to last p worked)5-1 + (j to center p of ring 6 of center flower motif)8-3.

Head: S1: R3 + (j to last p worked)1 + (j to next center p of ring 5 of center flower motif)1-3.

Right large wing: S1: R3 + (j to last p worked)8 + (j to center p of ring 4 of center flower motif)1 + (j to center p of last DR worked on half daisy)5 + (j to SR p of right small wing)3. End off.

Left Side:

Using CTM wind two shuttles.

S1: R2-1-1-2 + (j to third p of left small wing of Butterfly Point)2-1-1-2.

Half Daisy:

SR S1: R2-1-1-2, S2: LHK 3-3.

RW DR S2: R3 + (j to last p worked)3 + (j to p of left large wing of Butterfly Point)3-3.

S2: R3 + (j to last p worked)3 + (j to center p of ring 7 of center flower motif)3-3.

S2: R3 + (j to last p worked)3 + (j to center p of right large wing of Butterfly A)3-3. **RW**

SR S1: R2-1-1-2, using *shuttle three* LHK 3 + (j to base of center DR)3. End off S3.

SR S1: R2-1-1-2, S2: LHK 3 + (j to p of last DR worked)3.

SR S1: R2-1-1-2, S2: LHK 2-1-1-2. Repeat once.

SR S1: R2-1-1-2, S2: LHK 3 + (j to center p of right small wing)3.

SR S1: R2-1-1-2, S2: LHK 2-1-1-2.

SR S1: R2-1-1-2, S2: LHK 3 + (j to center p of butterfly's butt)3.

SR S1: R2-1-1-2, S2: LHK 2-1-1-2.

SR S1: R2-1-1-2, S2: LHK 3 + (j to center p of left small wing)3.

SR S1: R2-1-1-2, S2: LHK 6.

SR S1: R2-1-1-2, S2: LHK 6. End off. Join to base of first ring.

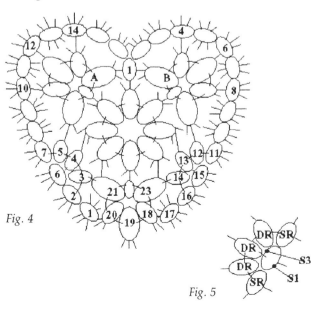

Fig. 4

Fig. 5

To My Heart's Content

Intermediate skill level.
Materials: 2 shuttles, Size 20-gauge 3-ply thread.

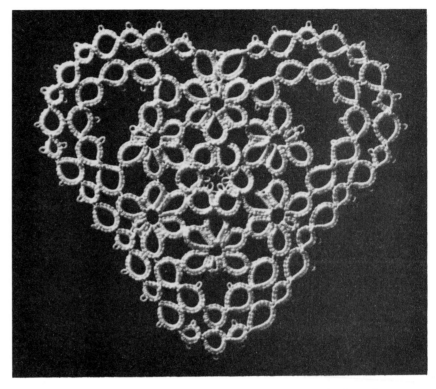

Center Split Rings *(Fig. 1)*

Using CTM wind two shuttles.
Sl: R10-3-1-1-3.
SR Sl: R3 + (j to last p worked)1-1-3, S2: LHK 10.
  Repeat 3x more.
SR S1: R3 + (j to last p worked)1-1 + (j to second p worked of first R)3 + (j to first p worked of first ring), S2: LHK 10. Do not end off. (6 split rings total)

You will now climb out of the center ring by tatting the first butterfly motif.
Butterfly butt: SR S1: R5-5, S2: LHK 5-5.
Left small wing: Sl: R5 + (j to first p worked of split ring)3-5-3.
Left large wing: Sl: R3 + (j to last p worked)5-7-3.
Head: Sl: R3 + (j to last p worked)1-1-3.
Right large wing: Sl: R3 + (j to last p worked)7-5-3.
Right small wing: Sl: R3 + (j to last p worked)5-3 + (j to LHK p worked of split ring)5. End off.

Butterfly Motifs *(Figs. 2 & 3)*

Wind one shuttle only.
Join butterfly motifs clockwise.
Butt: R5-5 + (j to space between split rings)5-5.

Left small wing: R5 + (j to last p worked)3 + (j to corresponding p of prior right small wing)5-3.
Left large wing: R3 + (j to last p worked)5-7-3.
Head: R3 + (j to last p worked)1-1-3.
Right large wing: R3 + (j to last p worked)7-5-3.
Right small wing: R3 + (j to last p worked)5-3 + (j to first p worked of butt)5. End off.
Repeat butterfly motif pattern 3x more.

For last butterfly (E), repeat pattern above, tatting the last wing as follows: R3 + (j to last p worked)5 + (j to corresponding p of climbing-out butterfly's wing)3 + (j to first p worked of butt)5. End off.

Heart Point Inner Split Ring Border

(Fig. 4)

Using CTM wind two shuttles.
Sl: R5 + (j to left large wing of butterfly C)5 + (j to right large wing of butterfly B)5-5.
SR Sl: R5-5, S2: LHK 5-5.
Corner point: SR S1: R5-5, S2: LHK 5.
SR S1: R5-5, S2: LHK 5-5.
S1: R5-5 + (j to left large wing of butterfly D)5 + (j to right large wing of butterfly C)5. End off.

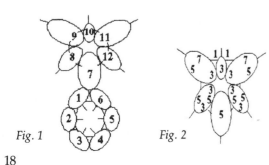

Fig. 1   *Fig. 2*

climbing out

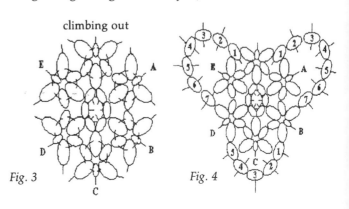

Fig. 3   *Fig. 4*

18

Heart Right Inner Split Ring Border

(Fig. 4)

Using CTM wind two shuttles.

S1: R5 + (j to left large wing of butterfly A)5-5 + (j to right large wing of climbing-out butterfly)5.

SR Sl: R5-5, S2: LHK 5-5. Repeat 4x more. (6 rings total)

S1: R5-5 + (j to left large wing of butterfly B)5 + (j to right large wing of butterfly A)5. End off.

Heart Left Inner Split Ring Border

(Fig. 4)

Using CTM wind two shuttles.

S1: R5 + (j to left large wing of climbing-out butterfly)5-5 + (j to right large wing of butterfly E)5.

SR S1: R5-5, S2: LHK 5-5. Repeat 4x more. (6 rings total)

S1: R5 + (j to left large wing of butterfly E)5 + (j to right large wing of butterfly D)5-5. End off.

Outer Cameo Split Ring Border *(Fig. 5)*

Using CTM wind two shuttles.

S1: R10 + (j to top of climbing-out butterfly's head)5-5.

SR S1: R3-3, S2: LHK 3-3.

SR S1: R5-5, S2: LHK 5 + (j to ring 2 of right inner split ring border)5.

SR S1: R3-3, S2: LHK 3-3.

*SR S1: R5-5, S2: LHK 5 + (j to next ring of right inner split ring border)5.

SR S1: R3-3, S2: LHK 3-3.* Repeat 2x more.

SR S1: R5-5, S2: LHK 5 + (j to ring 6)5.

SR S1: R3-3, S2: LHK 3 + (j to ring 7)3.

SR S1: R5-5, S2: LHK 10.

SR S1: R3-3, S2: LHK 3 + (j to top of butterfly B's head)3.

SR S1: R5-5, S2: LHK 10.

SR S1: R3-3, S2: LHK 3 + (j to ring 1 of inner split ring border)3.

SR S1: R5-5, S2: LHK 5 + (j to ring 2)5.

SR S1: R3-3, S2: LHK 3-3.

Corner point: SR S1: R5-5, S2: LHK 3 + (j to ring 3)3.

SR S1: R3-3, S2: LHK 3-3.

SR S1: R5-5, S2: LHK 5 + (j to ring 4)5.

SR S1: R3-3, S2: LHK 3 + (j to ring 5)3.

SR S1: R5-5, S2: LHK 10.

SR S1: R3-3, S2: LHK 3 + (j to butterfly D's head)3.

SR S1: R5-5, S2: LHK 10.

SR S1: R3-3, S2: LHK 3 + (j to ring 7 of left inner split ring border)3.

*SR S1: R5-5, S2: LHK 5 + (j to next ring of left inner split ring border)5.

SR S1: R3-3, S2: LHK 3-3.* Repeat 4x more.

S1: R5-5 + (j to climbing-out butterfly's head)10. End off.

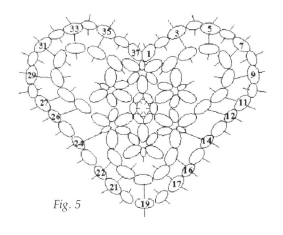

Fig. 5

Heartfelt

Intermediate skill level.

Materials: 2 shuttles, Size 20-gauge 3-ply thread.

Bottom Butterfly Motif *(Fig. 1)*

Wind one shuttle only.

Butterfly butt: R5-5-5-5.

Left small wing: R5 + (j to last p worked)3-5-3.

Left large wing: R3 + (j to last p worked)3-2-7-3.

Head: R3 + (j to last p worked)1-1-3.

Right large wing: R3 + (j to last p worked)7-2-3-3.

Right small wing: R3 + (j to last p worked)5-3 + (j to first p worked of butterfly butt)5. End off.

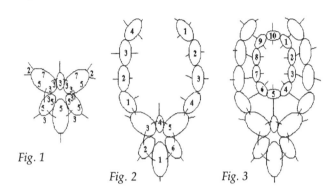

Fig. 1   *Fig. 2*   *Fig. 3*

Side Split Rings *(Fig. 2)*

Using CTM wind two shuttles.

Right Side:

S1: R5-5-5-5.

SR S1: R5-5, S2: LHK 5-5. Repeat once more.

S1: R10 + (j to bottom butterfly motif's right large wing)5-5. End off.

Left Side:

S1: R5-5 + (j to bottom butterfly motif's left large wing)10.

SR S1: R5-5, S2: LHK 5-5. Repeat once more.

S1: R5-5-5-5. End off.

Inner Split Ring Oval *(Fig. 3)*

Using CTM wind two shuttles.

S1: R3-3-3 + (j to inner p of first split ring of right side split rings)3.

SR S1: R3 + (j to next split ring p)3, S2: LHK 3-3. Repeat 2x more.

SR S1: R3 + (j to p of bottom butterfly's head)3, S2: LHK 3-3.

SR S1: R3 + (j to next split ring p)3, S2: LHK 3-3. Repeat 3x more.

SR S1: R3-3, S2: LHK 3-3. (10 split rings total) End off. Join to second p of first ring.

Side Butterfly Motifs *(Fig. 4)*

Wind one shuttle only.

Right Motif:

Butterfly butt: R5-5-5-5.

Left small wing: R5 + (j to last p worked)3-5-3.

Left large wing: R3 + (j to last p worked)9 + (j to second ring of right side split rings)3-3.

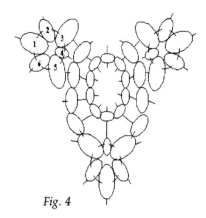

Fig. 4

Head: R3 + (j to last p worked)1-1-3.

Right large wing: R3 + (j to last p worked)3 + (j to first ring of right side split rings)9-3.

Right small wing: R3 + (j to last p worked)5-3 + (j to first p worked of butterfly's butt)5. End off.

Left Motif:

Butterfly butt: R5-5-5-5.

Left small wing: R5 + (j to last p worked)3-5-3.

Left large wing: R3 + (j to last p worked)9 + (j to last ring of left side split rings)3-3.

Head: R3 + (j to last p worked)1-1-3.

Right large wing: R3 + (j to last p worked)3 + (j to next ring of left side split rings)9-3.

Right small wing: R3 + (j to last p worked)5-3 + (j to first p worked of butterfly's butt)5. End off.

Heart Border *(Fig. 5)*

Using CTM wind two shuttles.

With a slip stitch, attach thread to p of bottom butterfly's butt.

Chain RDS 3-3-3-3 + (j with a lock stitch to p of right small wing)3-3-3-3.

R10 + (j to right large wing)10.

Chain RDS 3-3-3-3.

R10 + (j to p of next split ring of right side split rings)10.

Chain RDS 3-3-3-3.

R10 + (j to left small wing of right side butterfly)10.

Chain RDS 3-3-3-3.

R10 + (j to butterfly's butt)5-5.

Chain RDS 3-3-3-3.

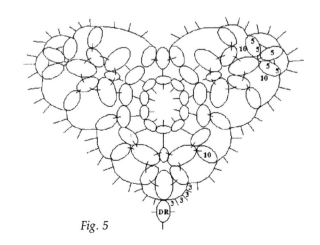

Fig. 5

R5 + (j to last p worked of prior ring)5 + (j to same p of butterfly's butt)5-5.
Chain RDS 3-3-3-3.
R5 + (j to last p worked of prior ring)5 + (j to same p of butterfly's butt)10.
Chain RDS 3-3-3-3.
R10 + (j to right small wing)10.
Chain RDS 3-3-3-3.

Clover:
R10 + (j to first ring of right side split rings)5-5.
R5 + (j to last p worked)5 + (j to p of inner split ring oval)5-5.
R5 + (j to last p worked)5 + (j to last ring of left side split rings)10.

Chain RDS 3-3-3-3.
R10 + (j to left small wing of left side butterfly)10.

Chain RDS 3-3-3-3.
R10 + (j to butterfly's butt)5-5.
Chain RDS 3-3-3-3.
R5 + (j to last p of prior ring)5 + (j to same p of butterfly's butt)5-5.
Chain RDS 3-3-3-3.
R5 + (j to last p of prior ring)5 + (j to same p of butterfly's butt)10.
Chain RDS 3-3-3-3.
R10 + (j to right small wing)10.
Chain RDS 3-3-3-3.
R10 + (j to p of next ring of left side split rings)10.
Chain RDS 3-3-3-3.
R10 + (j to left large wing)10.
Chain RDS 3-3-3-3 + (j with a lock stitch to left small wing)3-3-3-3 + (j with a lock stitch to butterfly's butt).
RW DR S2: R5-3-3-5. **RW** End off.

Cupid's Heart

Intermediate skill level.
Materials: 2 shuttles,
   Size 20-gauge 3-ply thread.

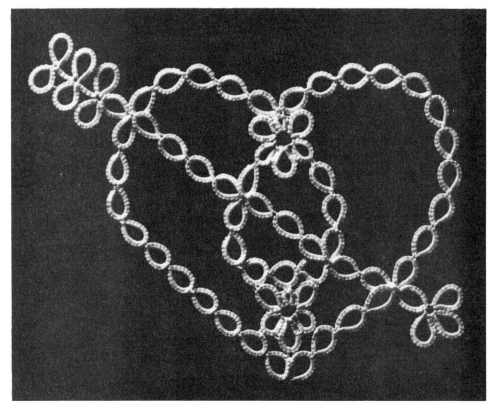

Bottom Butterfly Motif *(Fig. 1)*
Wind one shuttle only.
Butt: R5-5-5-5.
Left small wing: R5 + (j to last p worked)3-5-3.
Left large wing: R3 + (j to last p worked)5-7-3.
Head: R3 + (j to last p worked)1-1-3.
Right large wing: R3 + (j to last p worked)7-5-3.
Right small wing: R3 + (j to last p worked)5-3 + (j to first p worked of butt)5. End off.

Chained Butterfly *(Fig. 2)*
Using CTM wind two shuttles.
S1: R10-10.
SR S1: R10, S2: LHK 10. Repeat once more.

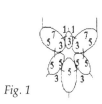

Fig. 1

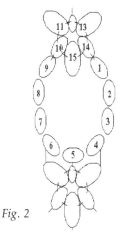

Fig. 2

21

SR S1: R5 + (j to right large wing of bottom butterfly)5, S2: LHK 10.
SR S1: R5 + (j to bottom butterfly's head)5, S2: LHK 10.
SR S1: R5 + (j to left large wing)5, S2: LHK 10.
SR S1: R10, S2: LHK 10. Repeat 2x more.

Butterfly:
Left small wing: SR S1: R5-3, S2: LHK 3-5.
Left large wing: S1: R3 + (j to S1 p of split ring)12-3.
Head: S1: R3 + (j to last p worked)1-1-3.
Right large wing: S1: R3 + (j to last p worked)12-3.
Right small wing: S1: R3 + (j to last p worked)5 + (j to first split ring of chain)3-5.
Butt: S1: R5 + (j to last p worked)10 + (j to LHK p of left small wing)5. End off.

Heart Chain Border (*Fig. 3*)
Using CTM wind two shuttles.
S1: R10 + (j to chained butterfly's head)10.
SR S1: R10, S2: LHK 10. Repeat 11x more.
SR S1: R10, S2: LHK 5 + (j to right small wing of bottom butterfly)5.
SR S1: R10, S2: LHK 5 + (j to p of butt)5.
SR S1: R10, S2: LHK 5 + (j to same p of butt)5.
SR S1: R10, S2: LHK 5 + (j to left small wing)5.
SR S1: R10, S2: LHK 10. Repeat 11x more.
S1: R10 + (j to chained butterfly's head)10. End off.

Cupid's Arrow (*Fig. 4*)
Using CTM wind two shuttles.
S1: R15-5.
RW DR S2: R15-5. **RW**
Chain RDS 5.
S1: R5 + (j to last p of prior S1 ring)10-5.
RW DR S2: R5 + (j to last p of prior S2 ring)10-5. **RW**
Chain RDS 5.
S1: R5 + (j to last p of prior S1 ring)15.
RW DR S2: R5 + (j to last p of prior S2 ring)15. **RW**
SR S1: R10, S2: LHK 10.
Counting back from end of heart chain border, bring S1 over and S2 under the border between the fifth and sixth SR.
SR S1: R10, S2: LHK 10. Repeat 3x more. (4 SR total)
Counting back from the end of chained butterfly, bring S1 over and S2 under between the first and second SR.
SR S1: R10, S2: LHK 10. Repeat 2x more. (3 SR total)
Counting back from end of chained butterfly, bring S1 over and S2 under between the sixth and seventh SR.
SR S1: R10, S2: LHK 10. Repeat once more.
Counting back from end of heart chain border, bring S1 over and S2 under between the nineteenth and twentieth SR.
SR S1: R10, S2: LHK 10.
Clover point: S1: R15-5.
S1: R5 + (j to last p worked)5-5-5.
S1: R5 + (j to last p worked)15. End off.

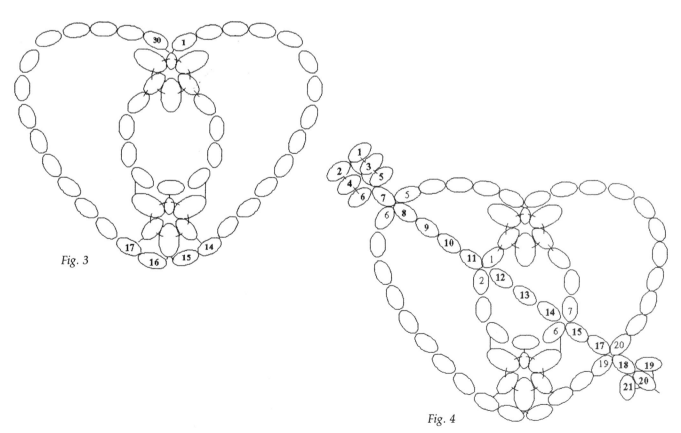

Fig. 3

Fig. 4

Gypsy Heart

Intermediate skill level.
Materials: 2 shuttles,
    Size 20-gauge 3-ply thread.

Center Motif *(Fig. 1)*

Using CTM wind two shuttles.
S1: R5-5-3-1-1-3.
*SR S1: R3 + (j to corresponding p of previous ring)1-1-3,
   S2: LHK 5-5.* Repeat 5x more.
SR S1: R3 + (j to corresponding p)1-1 + (j to correspond-
   ing p of first ring)3 + (j to second p of first ring), S2:
   LHK 5-5. End off. (8 rings total)

Cameo Split Rings *(Fig. 2)*

Using CTM wind two shuttles.
S1: R5 + (j to p of ring 1 of center motif)5-5-5.
SR S1: R3-3, S2: LHK 3-3.
SR S1: R5-5, S2: LHK 5 + (j to p of ring 2 of center
   motif)5.
SR S1: R3-3, S2: LHK 3-3.
*SR S1: R5-5, S2: LHK 5 + (j to p of next ring of center
   motif)5.
SR S1: R3-3, S2: LHK 3-3.* Repeat 5x. End off. Join to
   second picot of first ring. (16 rings total)

Butterfly A Motif *(Fig. 2)*

Wind one shuttle only.
Butt: R5-5-5-5.
Left small wing: R5 + (j to last p worked)3-5-3.
Left large wing: R3 + (j to last p worked)5-4 + (j to ring 10
   of cameo split rings)4-3.
Head: R3 + (j to last p worked)1 + (j to ring 9 of cameo
   split rings)1-3.
Right large wing: R3 + (j to last p worked)4 + (j to ring 8
   of cameo split rings)4-5-3.
Right small wing: R3 + (j to last p worked)5-3 + (j to first
   p of butt)5. End off.

Chained Butterflies

Using CTM wind two shuttles.

Right Side *(Fig. 3)*:
S1: R3-3 + (j to right large wing of bottom butterfly)3-3.
SR S1: R5 + (j to ring 7 of cameo rings)5, S2: LHK 5-5.
SR S1: R3-3, S2: LHK 3-3.

Butterfly B:
Butt: SR S1: R5-5, S2: LHK 5-5.
Left small wing: S1: R5 + (j to last S1 p worked)3 + (j to
   ring 5 of cameo rings)5-3.
Left large wing: S1: R3 + (j to last p worked)5-7-3.
Right small wing: **RW DR** S2: R5 + (j to last LHK p
   worked)3-5-3.
Right large wing: S2: R3 + (j to last p worked)5-7-3. **RW**
Head: SR S1: R3 + (j to last S1 p worked)1, S2: LHK 3 + (j
   to last S2 p worked)1.

SR S1: R3-3, S2: LHK 3-3.

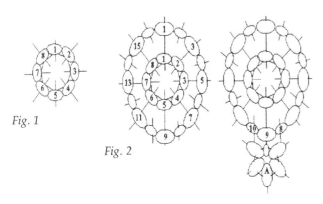

Fig. 1

Fig. 2

23

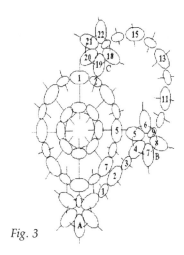

Fig. 3

*SR S1: R5-5, S2: LHK 5-5.
SR S1: R3-3, S2: LHK 3-3.* Repeat 2x.

Butterfly C:
Head: SR S1: R1-3, S2: LHK 1-3.
Right large wing: Sl: R3 + (j to S1 p)7-5-3.
Right small wing: S1: R3 + (j to last p worked)5 + (j to ring 2 of cameo rings)3-5.
Butt: S1: R5 + (j to last p worked)5 + (j to ring 1 of cameo rings)5-5.
Left small wing: Sl: R5 + (j to last p worked)3-5-3.
Left large wing: S1: R3 + (j to last p worked)5-7 + (j to LHK p of head)3. End off.

Left Side *(Fig. 4)*:
S1: R3-3 + (j to left large wing of bottom butterfly)3-3.
SR S1: R5-5, S2: LHK 5 + (j to ring 11 of cameo ring)5.
SR S1: R3-3, S2: LHK 3-3.

Butterfly D:
Butt: SR S1: R5-5, S2: LHK 5-5.
Left small wing: Sl: R5 + (j to last Sl p worked)3-5-3.
Left large wing: S1: R3 + (j to last p worked)5-7-3.
Right small wing: **RW DR** S2: R5 + (j to last LHK p worked)3 + (j to ring 13 of cameo rings)5-3.
Right large wing: S2: R3 + (j to last p worked)5-7-3. **RW**
Head: SR S1: R3 + (j to last S1 p worked)1, S2: LHK 3 + (j to last S2 p worked)1.

*SR S1: R3-3, S2: LHK 3-3.
SR S1: R5-5, S2: LHK 5-5.* Repeat 2x.
SR S1: R3-3, S2: LHK 3-3.

Butterfly E:
Head: SR S1: R1-3, S2: LHK 1-3.
Right large wing: Sl: R3 + (j to Sl p of head)7-5-3.
Right small wing: S1: R3 + (j to last p worked)5 + (j to left small wing of butterfly C)3-5.
Butt: S1: R5 + (j to last p worked)5 + (j to ring 1 of cameo rings)5-5.
Left small wing: Sl: R5 + (j to last p worked)3 + (j to ring 16 of cameo rings)5-3.
Left large wing: S1: R3 + (j to last p worked)5-7 + (j to LHK p)3. End off.

Split Ring Border *(Fig. 4)*
Using CTM wind two shuttles.

Right Side:
S1: R5-5-5 + (j to butt of butterfly A)5.
SR S1: R3-3, S2: LHK 3-3.
SR S1: R5 + (j to right small wing of butterfly A)5, S2: LHK 5-5.
SR S1: R3-3, S2: LHK 3-3.
SR S1: R5 + (j to ring 2 of right-side chained butterflies)5, S2: LHK 5-5.
SR S1: R3-3, S2: LHK 3-3.
SR S1: R5 + (j to right small wing of butterfly B)5, S2: LHK 5-5.
SR S1: R3 + (j to right large wing of butterfly B)3, S2: LHK 3-3.
*SR S1: R5-5, S2: LHK 5-5.
SR S1: R3-3, S2: LHK 3-3.* Repeat 4x.
SR S1: R5-5, S2: LHK 5-5. End off. Join in left large wing of butterfly C.

Left Side:
S1: R3-3 + (j in second p, first ring of border split rings)3-3.
SR S1: R5-5, S2: LHK 5 + (j to left small wing of butterfly A)5.
SR S1: R3-3, S2: LHK 3-3.
SR S1: R5-5, S2: LHK 5 + (j to ring 2 of left-side chained butterflies)5.
SR S1: R3-3, S2: LHK 3-3.
SR S1: R5-5, S2: LHK 5 + (j to left small wing of butterfly D)5.
SR S1: R3-3, S2: LHK 3 + (j to left large wing of butterfly D)3.
*SR S1: R5-5, S2: LHK 5-5.
SR S1: R3-3, S2: LHK 3-3.* Repeat 4x.
SR S1: R5-5, S2: LHK 5-5. End off. Join in wing of butterfly E.

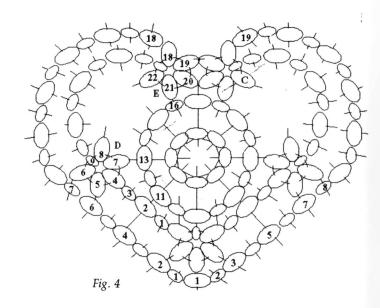

Fig. 4

Heart Frame

Intermediate/advanced skill level.
Materials: 2 shuttles, Size 20-gauge 3-ply thread.

Frame *(Figs. 1 and 2)*
Using CTM wind two shuttles.

Bottom Clover Point:
S1: R3-5-3.
S1: R3 + (j to last p worked)5-5-3.
S1: R3 + (j to last p worked)5-3.

Chain RDS 3.
S1: R3 + (j to last p worked)5-3.
RW DR S2: R3-5-3. **RW**
*Chain RDS 3.
S1:R3 + (j to corresponding p of last S1 ring)5-3.
RW DR S2: R3 + (j to corresponding p of last S2 ring)5-3. **RW*** Repeat 5x more.
*Chain RDS 3.
S1: R3 + (j to corresponding p)7-3.
RW DR S2: R3 + (j to corresponding p)3-3. **RW*** Repeat 6x more.
*Chain RDS 3.
S1: R3 + (j to corresponding p)5-3.
RW DR S2: R3 + (j to corresponding p)3-3. **RW*** Repeat once more.

Top Clover Point:
Chain RDS 5.
RW DR S2: R3 + (j to corresponding p)5-3.
S2: R3 + (j to last p worked)5-5-3.
S2: R3 + (j to last p worked)5-3. **RW**

Chain RDS 5.
*S1: R3 + (j to corresponding p)5-3.
RW DR S2: R3 + (j to corresponding p)3-3. **RW**
Chain RDS 3.* Repeat once more.
*S1: R3 + (j to corresponding p)7-3.
RW DR S2: R3 + (j to corresponding p)3-3. **RW**
Chain RDS 3.* Repeat 6x more.
*S1: R3 + (j to corresponding p)5-3.
RW DR S2: R3 + (j to corresponding p)5-3. **RW**
Chain RDS 3.* Repeat 6x more.
S1: R3 + (j to corresponding p)5 + (j to corresponding p of Bottom Clover Point)3.
RW DR S2: R3 + (j to corresponding p)5 + (j to first DR)3. **RW**
Chain RDS 3. Join in base of second ring of Bottom Clover Point. End off.

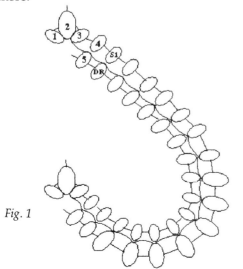

Fig. 1

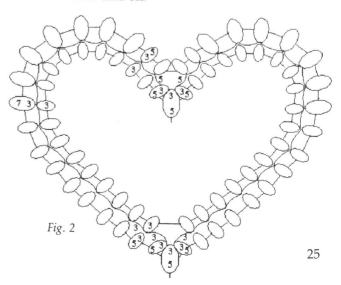

Fig. 2

Heartbreaker

Advanced skill level.
Materials: 2 shuttles,
    Size 20-gauge 3-ply thread.

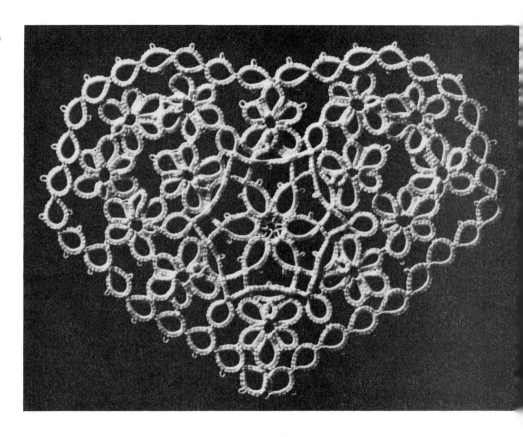

Center Rings *(Fig. 1)*

Using CTM wind two shuttles.
S1: R3-5-3-1-1-3-5-3.
*Chain RDS 5-5.
Butterfly's head: **RW DR** S2: R1-6-1. **RW**
Chain RDS 5-5.
S1: R3-5 + (j to next to last p of S1 ring)3 + (j to next p of same ring)1-1-3-5-3.* Repeat 3x.
Chain RDS 5-5.
RW DR S2: R1-6-1. **RW**
Chain RDS 5-5.
S1: R3-5 + (j to next to last p of last S1 ring)3 + (j to next p of same ring)1-1 + (j to third p of first S1 ring)3 + (j to second p of first S1 R)5-3.
Chain RDS 5-5.
RW DR S2: R1-6-1. **RW**
Chain RDS 5-5. End off. Join in base of first ring.

Butterfly Motifs *(Fig. 2)*

Wind one shuttle only.
Butterfly butt: R5-5-5-5.
Left small wing: R5 + (j to last p worked)3-5-3.
Left large wing: R3 + (j to last p worked)5-4 + (j to p of chain to the left of any head ring on center rings)3 + (j to p of head ring)3.
Right large wing: R3 + (j to head ring)3 + (j to p of chain)4-5-3.
Right small wing: R3 + (j to last p worked)5-3 + (j to first p of butt)5. End off.
Repeat motif 5x more.

Overlapping Chain *(Fig. 3)*

Wind shuttle; cut thread, leaving about 2 yards free for "ball thread."

R3 + (j to left large wing of butterfly A)7-7 + (j to right large wing of butterfly B)3.
Chain RDS 5.

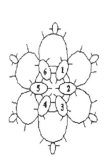

Fig. 1

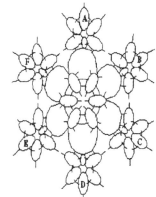

Fig. 2

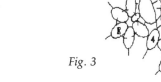

Fig. 3

Slip ball thread behind previous tatted chain from center rings.

Chain RDS 5-5.

Slip ball thread behind previous tatted chain from center rings.

Chain RDS 5.

R3 + (j to left large wing of butterfly B)7-7 + (j to right large wing of butterfly C)3.

Chain RDS 5.

Slip ball thread behind previous tatted chain from center rings.

Chain RDS 5-5.

Slip ball thread behind previous tatted chain from center rings.

Chain RDS 5.

*R3 + (j to left large wing of same butterfly)7-7 + (j to right large wing of next butterfly)3.

Chain RDS 5.

Slip ball thread behind previous tatted chain from center rings.

Chain RDS 5-5.

Slip ball thread behind previous tatted chain from center rings.

Chain RDS 5.* Repeat 2x.

R3 + (j to left large wing of butterfly F)7-7 + (j to right large wing of butterfly A)3.

Chain RDS 5.

Slip ball thread behind previous tatted chain from center rings.

Chain RDS 5-5.

Slip ball thread behind previous tatted chain from center rings.

Chain RDS 5. End off. Connect chain in base of first ring.

Joined Butterflies *(Fig. 4)*

Using CTM wind two shuttles.

Right Side:

Butterfly one:

Butt: S1: R5-5 + (j to center p of first ring worked on overlapping chain)5-5.

Left small wing: S1: R5 + (j to last p worked)3-5-3.

Left large wing: S1: R3 + (j to last p worked)5-7-3.

Right small wing: **RW DR** S2: R5 + (j to corresponding p of prior ring)3 + (j to right small wing of butterfly B)5-3.

Right large wing: S2: R3 + (j to last p worked)5-7-3. **RW**

Head: SR S1: R3 + (j to p of S1 ring)1, S2: LHK 3 + (j to p of S2 ring)1.

Butterfly two:

Butt: SR S1: R5-5, S2: LHK 5-5.

Left small wing: S1: R5 + (j to last p worked)3-5-3.

Left large wing: S1: R3 + (j to last p worked)5-7-3.

Right small wing: **RW DR** S2: R5 + (j to corresponding p of prior ring)3 + (j to right large wing of last butterfly worked)5-3.

Right large wing: S2: R3 + (j to last p worked)5-7-3. **RW**

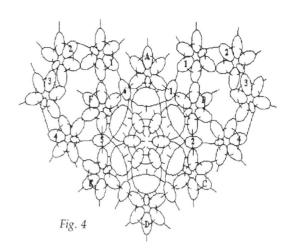

Fig. 4

Head: SR S1: R3 + (j to p of S1 ring)1, S2: LHK 3 + (j to p of S2 ring)1.

Butterfly three:

Butt: SR S1: R5-5, S2: LHK 5-5.

Left small wing: S1: R5 + (j to last p worked)3-5-3.

Left large wing: S1: R3 + (j to last p worked)5-7-3.

Right small wing: **RW DR** S2: R5 + (j to corresponding p of prior ring)3 + (j to right large wing of last butterfly worked)5-3.

Right large wing: S2: R3 + (j to last p worked)5-7-3. **RW**

Head: SR S1: R3 + (j to p of S1 ring)1, S2: LHK 3 + (j to p of S2 ring)1.

Butterfly four:

Butt: SR S1: R5-5, S2: LHK 5-5.

Left small wing: S1: R5 + (j to last p worked)3-5-3.

Left large wing: Sl: R3 + (j to last p worked)5-4 + (j to right small wing of butterfly C)3-3.

Head: S1: R3 + (j to last p worked)1 + (j to second ring of overlapping chain)1-3.

Right large wing: S1: R3 + (j to last p worked)7 + (j to left small wing of butterfly B)5-3.

Right small wing: S1: R3 + (j to last p worked)5 + (j to right large wing of last butterfly worked)3 + (j to last LHK p of last SR worked)5. End off.

Left Side:

Using CTM wind two shuttles.

Butterfly one:

Butt: S1: R5-5 + (j to center p of sixth ring worked on overlapping chain)5-5.

Left small wing: S1: R5 + (j to last p worked)3 + (j to p of left small wing of butterfly F)5-3.

Left large wing: S1: R3 + (j to last p worked)5-7-3.

Right small wing: **RW DR** S2: R5 + (j to corresponding p of prior ring)3-5-3.

Right large wing: S2: R3 + (j to last S1 p worked)5-7-3. **RW**

Head: SR S1: R3 + (j to p of S1 ring)1, S2: LHK 3 + (j to p of S2 ring)1.

Butterfly two:

Butt: SR S1: R5-5, S2: LHK 5-5.

Left small wing: S1: R5 + (j to last p worked)3 + (j to left large wing of last butterfly)5-3.

27

Left large wing: S1: R3 + (j to last p worked)5-7-3.
Right small wing: **RW DR** S2: R5 + (j to corresponding p of prior ring)3-5-3.
Right large wing: S2: R3 + (j to last p worked)5-7-3. **RW**
Head: SR S1: R3 + (j to p of S1 ring)1, S2: LHK 3 + (j to p of S2 ring)1.

Butterfly three:
Butt: SR S1: R5-5, S2: LHK 5-5.
Left small wing: S1: R5 + (j to last p worked)3 + (j to left large wing of last butterfly)5-3.
Left large wing: S1: R3 + (j to last p worked)5-7-3.
Right small wing: **RW DR** S2: R5 + (j to corresponding p of prior ring)3-5-3.
Right large wing: S2: R3 + (j to last p worked)5-7-3. **RW**
Head: SR S1: R3 + (j to p of S1 ring)1, S2: LHK 3 + (j to p of S2 ring)1.

Butterfly four:
Butt: SR S1: R5-5, S2: LHK 5-5.
Left small wing: S1: R5 + (j to last S1 p worked)3 + (j to left large wing of last butterfly)5-3.
Left large wing: S1: R3 + (j to last p worked)5 + (j to right small wing of butterfly F)7-3.
Head: S1: R3 + (j to last p worked)1 + (j to fifth ring of overlapping chain)1-3.
Right large wing: S1: R3 + (j to last p worked)4 + (j to left small wing of butterfly E)3-5-3.
Right small wing: S1: R3 + (j to last p worked)5-3 + (j to LHK p of last SR worked)5. End off.

Split Ring Border *(Fig. 5)*
Using CTM wind two shuttles.
S1: R5-5 + (j to butt of butterfly A)5-5.
SR S1: R5-5, S2: LHK 5 + (j to left small wing of first butterfly on right side)5.
SR S1: R5-5, S2: LHK 5 + (j to left large wing)5.
SR S1: R5-5, S2: LHK 5-5.

SR S1: R5-5, S2: LHK 5 + (j to left small wing of next butterfly)5.
SR S1: R5-5, S2: LHK 5 + (j to left large wing)5.
SR S1: R5-5, S2: LHK 5-5.
SR S1: R5-5, S2: LHK 5 + (j to left small wing of next butterfly)5.
SR S1: R5-5, S2: LHK 5 + (j to left large wing)5.
SR S1: R5-5, S2: LHK 5-5.
SR S1: R5-5, S2: LHK 5-5.
SR S1: R5-5, S2: LHK 5 + (j to left small wing of next butterfly)5.
SR S1: R5-5, S2: LHK 5-5.
SR S1: R5-5, S2: LHK 5 + (j to butt of butterfly C)5.
SR S1: R5-5, S2: LHK 5 + (j to left small wing of butterfly C)5.
SR S1: R5-5, S2: LHK 5 + (j to third ring of overlapping chain)5.
SR S1: R5-5, S2: LHK 5 + (j to right small wing of butterfly D)5.
SR S1: R5-5, S2: LHK 5 + (j to butt of butterfly D)5.
SR S1: R5-5, S2: LHK 5 + (j to same p as last SR)5.
SR S1: R5-5, S2: LHK 5 + (j to left small wing of butterfly D)5.
SR S1: R5-5, S2: LHK 5 + (j to fourth ring of overlapping chain)5.
SR S1: R5-5, S2: LHK 5 + (j to right small wing of butterfly E)5.
SR S1: R5-5, S2: LHK 5 + (j to butt of butterfly E)5.
SR S1: R5-5, S2: LHK 5-5.
SR S1: R5-5, S2: LHK 5 + (j to right small wing of butterfly 4)5.
SR S1: R5-5, S2: LHK 5-5.
SR S1: R5-5, S2: LHK 5-5.
*SR S1: R5-5, S2: LHK 5 + (j to right large wing of next butterfly)5.
SR S1: R5-5, S2: LHK 5 + (j to right small wing)5.
SR S1: R5-5, S2: LHK 5-5.* Repeat 2x. End off. Connect to Butterfly A.

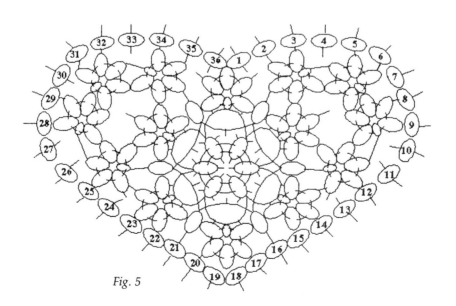

Fig. 5

Heart Blossom

Advanced skill level.
Materials: 3 shuttles,
Size 20-gauge 3-ply thread.

Center Wheel (Fig. 1)

Wind one shuttle.

R2-2-2-2-2-2-2-2. (7 picots)

Climb out of ring, leaving a space for a mock picot.

R5-5-5-5.

*Lock stitch in next p of center wheel. (Pull loop down through top of picot.)

R5 + (j in last p worked)5-5-5.* Repeat 5x more. Lock stitch in next p of center wheel.

R5 + (j in last p worked)5-5 + (j in first p of climb out ring)5. Lock stitch in mock picot of center wheel. End off. (8 rings total)

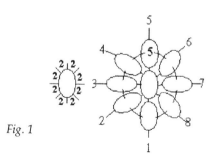

Fig. 1

Daisy Diamond (Fig. 2)

Using CTM wind two shuttles.

Daisy one:

R1 S1: R3-3-3-3.

R2 S1: R3 + (j to last p worked)3 + (j to ring 3 of center wheel)3-3.

S1: R3 + (j to last p worked)3-3-3. Repeat 4x more.

R8 SR Sl: R3 + (j to last p worked)3, S2: LHK 3 + (j to first p worked of first ring)3.

Daisy two:

R9 SR S1: R3-3, S2: LHK 3-3.

R10 S1: R3 + (j to S1 p)3-3-3.

S1: R3 + (j to last p worked)3-3-3. Repeat once more.

RW DR S2: R3 + (j to LHK p)3 + (j to center p, ring 1 of last daisy)3-3.

S2: R3 + (j to last p worked)3 + (j to center p, ring 4 of center wheel)3-3.

S2: R3 + (j to last p worked)3-3-3. **RW**

SR S1: R3 + (j to S1 of ring 12)3, S2: LHK 3 + (j to S2 p of ring 15)3.

Daisy three:

R17 SR S1: R3-3, S2: LHK 3-3.

R18 S1: R3 + (j to S1 p)3-3-3.

S1: R3 + (j to last p worked)3-3-3. Repeat once more.

RW DR S2: R3 + (j to LHK p)3 + (j to center p, ring 15 of last daisy)3-3.

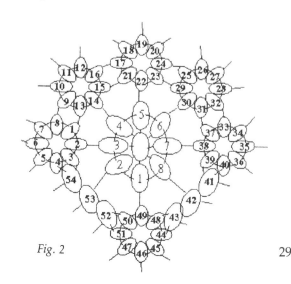

Fig. 2

29

S2: R3 + (j to last p worked)3 + (j to center p, ring 5 of center wheel)3-3.

S2: R3 + (j to last p worked)3-3-3. **RW**

SR S1: R3 + (j to S1 p of ring 20)3, S2: LHK 3 + (j to S2 p of ring 23)3.

Daisy four:

R25 SR S1: R3-3, S2: LHK 3-3.

R26 S1: R3 + (j to S1 p)3-3-3.

S1: R3 + (j to last p worked)3-3-3. Repeat once more.

RW DR S2: R3 + (j to LHK p)3 + (j to center p, ring 23 of last daisy)3-3.

S2: R3 + (j to last p worked)3 + (j to center p, ring 6 of center wheel)3-3.

S2: R3 + (j to last p worked)3-3-3. **RW**

SR S1: R3 + (j to S1 p of ring 28)3, S2: LHK 3 + (j to S2 p of ring 31)3.

Daisy five:

R33 SR S1: R3-3, S2: LHK 3-3

R34 S1: R3 + (j to S1 p)3-3-3.

S1: R3 + (j to last p worked)3-3-3. Repeat once more.

RW DR S2: R3 + (j to LHK p)3 + (j to center p, ring 31 of last daisy)3-3.

S2: R3 + (j to last p worked)3 + (j to center p, ring 7 of center wheel)3-3.

S2: R3 + (j to last p worked)3-3-3. **RW**

SR S1: R3 + (j to S1 p of ring 36)3, S2: LHK 3 + (j to S2 p of ring 39)3.

R41 SR S1: R5-5, S2: LHK 5 + (j to center p of ring 39)5.

SR S1: R5-5, S2: LHK 5 + (j to center p, ring 8 of center wheel)5.

SR S1: R5-5, S2: LHK 5-5.

Daisy six:

R44 SR S1: R3-3, S2: LHK 3-3.

R45 S1: R3 + (j to S1 p)3-3-3.

S1: R3 + (j to last p worked)3-3-3. Repeat once more.

RW DR S2: R3 + (j to last p worked)3 + (j to LHK p of ring 43)3-3.

S2: R3 + (j to last p worked)3 + (j to center p, ring 1 of center wheel)3-3.

S2: R3 + (j to LHK p)3-3-3. **RW**

SR S1: R3 + (j to S1 p of ring 47)3, S2: LHK 3 + (j to S2 p of ring 50)3.

R52 SR S1: R5-5, S2: LHK 5 + (j to center p of ring 50)5.

SR S1: R5-5, S2: LHK 5 + (j to center p, ring 2 of center wheel)5.

SR S1: R5-5, S2: LHK 5 + (j to center p, ring 3 of daisy one)5. End off. Join to center p, ring 4 of daisy one.

Split Ring Archs *(Fig. 3)*

Using CTM wind two shuttles.

Right Side:

S1: R5 + (j to center p of ring 26 of daisy four)5 + (j to space between rings 25 and 24 of daisies three and four)5 + (j to center p of ring 20 of daisy three)5.

SR S1: R5-5, S2: LHK 5-5. Repeat 4x more.

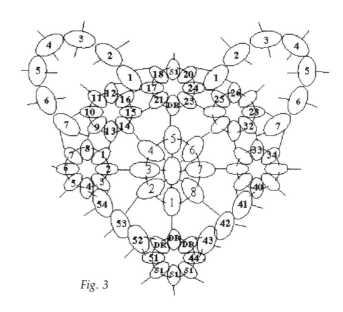

Fig. 3

SR S1: R5 + (j to center p, ring 34 of daisy five)5, S2: LHK 5 + (j to center p, ring 28 of daisy four)5. End off. Connect end to space between rings 32 and 33 of daisies four and five.

Left Side:

S1: R5 + (j to center p of ring 18 of daisy three)5 + (j to space between rings 16 and 17 of daisies two and three)5 + (j to center p of ring 12 of daisy two)5.

SR S1: R5-5, S2: LHK 5-5. Repeat 4x more.

SR S1: R5 + (j to center p, ring 10 of daisy two)5, S2: LHK 5 + (j to center p, ring 7 of daisy one)5. End off. Connect end to space between rings 8 and 9 of daisies one and two.

Heart Border *(Fig. 4)*

Using CTM wind two shuttles. Wind one shuttle separately.

Bottom Split Rings:

S1: R5-5-5 + (j to center p, ring 46 of daisy six)5.

SR S1: R5 + (j to center p, ring 45 of daisy six)5, S2: LHK 5-5.

SR S1: R5 + (j to center p, ring 43)5, S2: LHK 5-5.

SR S1: R5 + (j to center p, ring 42)5, S2: LHK 5-5.

SR S1: R5 + (j to center p, ring 41)5, S2: LHK 5-5.

SR S1: R5 + (j to center p, ring 36 of daisy five)5, S2: LHK 5-5.

Daisy one:

R7 SR S1: R3-3, S2: LHK 3-3.

R8 S1: R3 + (j to S1 p)3 + (j to center p, ring 35 of daisy five)3-3.

S1: R3 + (j to last p worked)3 + (j to center p, ring 34 of daisy five)3-3.

S1: R3 + (j to last p worked)3-3-3.

RW DR *S2: R3 + (j to last S2 p worked)3-3-3.* Repeat 2x more. **RW**

SR S1: R3 + (j to S1 p of ring 10)3, S2: LHK 3 + (j to S2 p of ring 13)3.

Daisy two:
R15 SR S1: R3-3, S2: LHK 3-3.
R16 S1: R3 + (j to S1 p)3 + (j to center p, ring 10 of last daisy)3-3.
S1: R3 + (j to last p worked)3 + (j to center p, ring 6 of split rings)3-3.
S1: R3 + (j to last p worked)3-3-3.
RW DR *S2: R3 + (j to last S2 p worked)3-3-3.* Repeat 2x more. **RW**
SR S1: R3 + (j to S1 p of ring 18), S2: LHK 3 + (j to S2 p of ring 21)3.

Daisy three:
R23 SR S1: R3-3, S2: LHK 3-3.
R24 S1: R3 + (j to S1 p)3 + (j to center p, ring 18 of last daisy)3-3.
S1: R3 + (j to last p worked)3 + (j to center p, ring 5 of split rings)3-3.
S1: R3 + (j to last p worked)3-3-3.
RW DR *S2: R3 + (j to last S2 p worked)3-3-3.* Repeat 2x more. **RW**
SR S1: R3 + (j to S1 p of ring 26), S2: LHK 3 + (j to S2 p of ring 29)3.

Daisy four:
R31 SR S1: R3-3, S2: LHK 3-3.
R32 S1: R3 + (j to S1 p)3 + (j to center p, ring 26 of last daisy)3-3.
S1: R3 + (j to last p worked)3 + (j to center p, ring 4 of split rings)3-3.
S1: R3 + (j to last p worked)3-3-3.
RW DR *S2: R3 + (j to last S2 p worked)3-3-3.* Repeat 2x more. **RW**
SR S1: R3 + (j to S1 p of ring 34), S2: LHK 3 + (j to S2 p of ring 37)3.

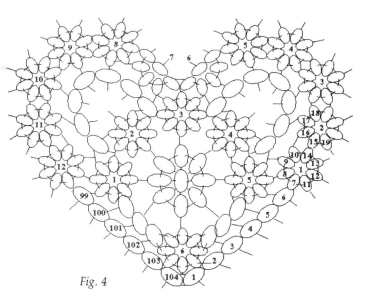

Fig. 4

Daisy five:
R39 SR S1: R3-3, S2: LHK 3-3.
R40 S1: R3 + (j to S1 p)3 + (j to center p, ring 34 of last daisy)3-3.
S1: R3 + (j to last p worked)3 + (j to center p, ring 3 of split rings)3-3.
S1: R3 + (j to last p worked)3-3-3.
RW DR *S2: R3 + (j to last S2 p worked)3-3-3.* Repeat 2x more. **RW**
SR S1: R3 + (j to S1 p of ring 42), S2: LHK 3 + (j to S2 p of ring 45)3.

Half Daisy six:
R47 SR S1: R3-3, S2: LHK 3-3.
R48 S1: R3 + (j to S1 p)3 + (j to center p, ring 42 of last daisy)3-3.
S1: R3 + (j to last p worked)3 + (j to center p, ring 2 of split rings)3-3.
S1: R3 + (j to last p worked)3 + (j to center p, ring 1 of split rings)3-3.
SR S2: R3 + (j to base of center S1 ring)3, S3: LHK 3-3. End off S3.
SR S1: R3 + (j to last p worked of ring 50)3, S2: LHK 3-3 + (j to center p, ring 19 of daisy three).

Half Daisy seven:
R53 SR S1: R3-3, S2: LHK 3 + (j to last LHK p of last split ring)3.
R54 S1: R3 + (j to S1 p)3 + (j to center p, ring 18 of daisy three)3-3.
S1: R3 + (j to last p worked)3 + (j to center p, ring 2 of split rings)3-3.
S1: R3 + (j to last p worked)3-3-3.
SR S2: R3 + (j to base of ring 55)3, S3: LHK 3-3. End off S3.
SR S1: R3 + (j to last p worked of ring 56)3, S2: LHK 3-3.

Daisy eight:
R59 SR S1: R3-3, S2: LHK 3-3.
R60 S1: R3 + (j to S1 p)3 + (j to center p, ring 56 of last daisy)3-3.
S1: R3 + (j to last p worked)3 + (j to center p, ring 3 of split rings)3-3.
S1: R3 + (j to last p worked)3-3-3.
RW DR *S2: R3 + (j to last S2 p worked)3-3-3.* Repeat 2x more. **RW**
SR S1: R3 + (j to S1 p of ring 62), S2: LHK 3 + (j to S2 p of ring 65)3.

Daisy nine:
R67 SR S1: R3-3, S2: LHK 3-3.
R68 S1: R3 + (j to S1 p)3 + (j to center p, ring 62 of last daisy)3-3.
S1: R3 + (j to last p worked)3 + (j to center p, ring 4 of split rings)3-3.
S1: R3 + (j to last p worked)3-3-3.

RW DR *S2: R3 + (j to last S2 p worked)3-3-3.* Repeat 2x more. **RW**

SR S1: R3 + (j to S1 p of ring 70), S2: LHK 3 + (j to S2 p of ring 72)3.

Daisy ten:

R75 SR S1: R3-3, S2: LHK 3-3.

R76 S1: R3 + (j to S1 p)3 + (j to center p, ring 70 of last daisy)3-3.

S1: R3 + (j to last p worked)3 + (j to center p, ring 5 of split rings)3-3.

S1: R3 + (j to last p worked)3-3-3.

RW DR *S2: R3 + (j to last S2 p worked)3-3-3.* Repeat 2x more. **RW**

SR S1: R3 + (j to S1 p of ring 78), S2: LHK 3 + (j to S2 p of ring 81)3.

Daisy eleven:

R83 SR S1: R3-3, S2: LHK 3-3.

R84 S1: R3 + (j to S1 p)3 + (j to center p, ring 78 of last daisy)3-3.

S1: R3 + (j to last p worked)3 + (j to center p, ring 6 of split rings)3-3.

S1: R3 + (j to last p worked)3-3-3.

RW DR *S2: R3 + (j to last S2 p worked)3-3-3.* Repeat 2x more. **RW**

SR S1: R3 + (j to S1 p of ring 86), S2: LHK 3 + (j to S2 p of ring 89)3.

Daisy twelve:

R91 SR S1: R3-3, S2: LHK 3-3.

R92 S1: R3 + (j to S1 p)3 + (j to center p, ring 86 of last daisy)3-3.

S1: R3 + (j to last p worked)3 + (j to center p, ring 7 of split rings)3-3.

S1: R3 + (j to last p worked)3 + (j to center p, ring 6 of daisy one)3-3.

RW DR *S2: R3 + (j to last S2 p worked)3-3-3.* Repeat 2x more. **RW**

SR S1: R3 + (j to S1 p of ring 94), S2: LHK 3 + (j to S2 p of ring 97)3.

Bottom Split Rings:

SR S1: R5 + (j to center p, ring 5 of daisy one)5, S2: LHK 5-5.

SR S1: R5 + (j to center p of ring 54)5, S2: LHK 5-5.

SR S1: R5 + (j to center p of ring 53)5, S2: LHK 5-5.

SR S1: R5 + (j to center p of ring 52)5, S2: LHK 5-5.

SR S1: R5 + (j to center p, ring 47 of daisy six)5, S2: LHK 5-5.

SR S1: R5 + (j to center p, ring 46 of daisy six)5, S2: LHK 5-5. End off. Join in second p of beginning ring.

Heart Mobile